RICHMOND
One of America's
BEST TENNIS TOWNS

By

Eric Perkins - Tom Hood - John Packett

**PUBLISHED BY
DEMENTI MILESTONE PUBLISHING**

First Printing

Copyright © 2012 by the Richmond Tennis Association

All rights reserved. No part of this book may be reproduced or transmitted in any form or by any means, electronically or mechanical, including photocopying, recording, or by any information storage and retrieval system, without the written permission of the Publisher.

Authors
Eric Perkins – Tom Hood – John Packett

Publisher
Wayne Dementi
Dementi Milestone Publishing, Inc.
Manakin-Sabot, VA 23103
www.dementimilestonepublishing.com

Cataloging-in-publication data for this book is available from The Library of Congress.
ISBN: 978-0-9838348-8-5

Graphic design by:
Dianne Dementi

Printed in USA

Attempts have been made to identify the owners of any copyrighted materials appearing in this book. The publisher extends his apology for any errors or omissions and encourages copyright owners inadvertently missed to contact him.

This is a production of Richmond Tennis Association, Inc., a Section 501(c)(3) charitable and educational organization dedicated to the promotion of tennis, sportsmanship, recreation and health throughout the Richmond area.

Table of Contents

Chapter 1 A Brief Chronology of Richmond Tennis
- The Early Years of Tennis in Richmond 1
- The Sam Woods Era (1940s-1950s) 5
- The Swingin' 60s 6
- The Booming 70s 9
- The Roaring 80s 14
- The Soaring 90s 16
- The 21st Century 19

Chapter 2 People, Teams and Programs
- Arthur Ashe 27
- Richmond Tennis Association 35
- Hall of Famers 43
- Richmond Tennis Notables 54
- Great High School Teams 55
- Great College Teams 59

Chapter 3 Places
- Public Parks 63
- Clubs 65
- Recreation Associations 72
- Arenas 76

Chapter 4 Events
- The City Tournament 79
- Virginia State Tennis Championships 84
- Virginia State Indoor Championships 88
- Mid-Atlantic Clay Court Championships 91
- "World's Largest Tennis Tournament" 94
- The Match They Thought Would Never End 96
- Charity Exhibitions 98
- Women's Pro Tour Comes to Richmond 101
- Richmond - Major Stop on the Men's Pro Tour 103
- Revenge of the Linesmen 107
- A Match to Remember 109
- Seniors Tour 111
- USTA Pro Circuit Events 113
- Ralph Whitaker Memorial 114
- Southeastern Open 115
- Davis Cup 116
- Cup Competitions 118
- Anthem Challenge 121

Chapter 5 The Present and Future of Richmond Tennis
- Best Tennis Town Contest 126
- Lobs & Lessons 128
- 10 and Under Tennis and the QuickStart Tennis Format 132

Introduction

Locals have long boasted that Richmond, Virginia is a great tennis town. Professional tournaments, exhibitions, nationally ranked college programs, record-setting high school tennis teams, award-winning tennis facilities, a talented array of innovative teaching professionals, a community tennis association with a successful track record of promoting tennis throughout the Richmond area for over fifty years, and thousands of active, enthusiastic tennis players of all ages and levels of play—all add up to compelling evidence to support those boasts.

In 2010, thanks to a USTA-sponsored national contest to determine the "Best Tennis Town" in America, we had our chance to showcase our tennis community, and that's exactly what we did. With its top-three finish and $25,000 prize, Richmond solidified its status as one of the best tennis towns in America and, in doing so, energized the entire community in ways that will yield dividends for years to come.

Amid the hoopla of the "Best Tennis Town" campaign, I met with Wayne Dementi, a friend and local tennis enthusiast known throughout Richmond for his family business "Dementi Studios" as well as an emerging presence in the publishing industry through Dementi Milestone Publishing, to discuss the potential of this project. We recruited renowned sports journalist John Packett and local tennis guru Tom Hood to join the effort. It was clear early on that we all shared the same vision for this project—that there are great stories and images that should be memorialized. Through this book, we can provide an educational and inspirational resource that could serve as a catalyst for people to make the decision to learn to play tennis or for a young person to realize that tennis could provide a path not only to a healthy, active lifestyle and an outlet for fun and fellowship with friends and family, but perhaps tennis could be a path to a college education or even a career. Even better, someone might read this book and realize—perhaps for the first time—that great things are possible when you diligently follow your passion and dreams.

This is a book about very special people, places, and events that over the course of many years have made, and continue today to make, Richmond one of America's best tennis towns.

Eric C. Perkins

Eric Perkins
Richmond Tennis Association President
(2004-2006, 2011)

Acknowledgments

The Richmond Tennis Association has been blessed to have the support of many dedicated volunteers whose efforts have advanced tennis in our community. We know we may have omitted some of these people and their achievements in writing this book, so please accept our apologies up front and know that your efforts are a valued part of Richmond tennis history.

This book would not have been possible without generous contributions, advice, feedback, recollections, scrapbook photos, newspaper clippings, tournament programs and assistance from the individuals and organizations listed below. Thank you very much.

Terry Aima
Romain Ambert
Bill Barnes
Martha Beddingfield
Randy Blunt
Bob Bortner
Ed Butterworth
Tom Cain
Tina Carter
Tom Chewning
Country Club of Virginia
Jack Cummings
Peggy Cummings
Lisa Deane
Jerry DePew
John DePew
Paul DiPasquale
Slater Dunbar
Sharon Dunsing
Lou Einwick
Michael and Elizabeth Fraizer
Rachel Gale
Bettty Gustafson
Rodney Harmon
Jean Hepner
Terry Hood
Waller Horsley
Tom Hoy
Rob Issem

Paul Kostin
Debbie Lahy
Carl and Cheryl Loden
P. J. Mahoney
Jim Milley
Heather Moon
Chris Mumford
Lee Mumford
Vicki Nelson Dunbar
Julie Ogborne
Eddie and Stacey Parker
Bill Redd
Bridget Reichert
Richmond Times-Dispatch
Cris and Melissa Robinson
John Royster
Damian Sancilio
Jolynn Johnson Smith
Joyce Steed
Scott Steinour
Sean Steinour
Shelley Stepp
William G. Thalhimer, III
Valentine Richmond History Center
Tony Velo
Virginia Historical Society
Guy Walton
Hugh Waters, III
Paddi Valentine Waters

The Richmond Tennis Association expresses its gratitude to its sponsors and patrons:

Grand Slam Patrons

Ed and Joy Fuhr
Anonymous

Corporate Sponsors

Association of Richmond Tennis Professionals
Davenport & Company LLC
Keiter (Carl Loden, Jay Nelson, Chris Wallace)
McDonald's
Metro Properties, Inc.
Raintree Swim & Racquet Club
Richmond Raiders LLC
The Westwood Club
Tuckahoe Orthopaedics
USTA/Virginia Tennis

Patrons

Fred and Mary Bruner
In Memory of Virginius Dabney (by Mr. and Mrs. Harold M. Burrows, Jr.)
The Caldwell Family
Matt and Jill Campbell
The Cofers (Eric, Carson & Conner)
Wayne and Dianne Dementi
Irving and Anne Driscoll
Drew Alexander Hendley
Tom and Terry Hood
Bob and Tracey Hughes
David and Fran Inge
Amy and Tracy Jones
Maggie Jones
The Donald and Debbie Lahy Family
In Memory of Bobby Leitch (by his children Rob, John and Anne Taylor)
Chris and Keith Mumford
Eddie and Stacey Parker
Marshall and Joyce Parker
Cheryl Perkins
Eric and Chrissie Perkins
Cris and Melissa Robinson
John Jay Schwartz
Bob and Kirsten Sell
Monty Stafford
Shelley Stepp
Larry Traylor
Hugh and Paddi Waters
Enid W. Weber
John and Margaret Whitlock
Jeff and Pam Wilson
Ginny Wortham
USTA/Mid-Atlantic Section
Three Chopt Recreation Club

John P. McEnroe, Jr.

John McEnroe is regarded by many as perhaps the most skilled—and controversial—tennis player of all time. Equally brilliant in singles and doubles (he won 155 pro titles in his legendary career—77 singles and 78 doubles), McEnroe was known for his strong serve, shot-making artistry, and competitive fire.

Born in Germany in 1959, where his father was stationed with the U.S. Air Force, John grew up in the Long Island suburb of Douglaston, NY, training with the legendary coach Harry Hopman and his right hand man, Tony Palafox, at Long Island's Port Washington Tennis Academy.

John won his first Grand Slam championship as a teenager, teaming with Mary Carillo to win the French Open mixed doubles title in 1977. He went on to win the U.S. Open four times (1979-81, 1984) and Wimbledon three times (1981, 1983-84), while ascending to the top of the world rankings in both singles and doubles (with Peter Fleming) and getting the better of both Borg and Connors in two of the most compelling rivalries in the modern era of tennis.

No American player appreciated the importance of Davis Cup more than John McEnroe, who led the U.S. team to the Davis Cup title on five different occasions and captained the U.S. squad in 2000. He still holds the record for most U.S. Davis Cup wins in singles (41) and in singles and doubles combined (59). John was inducted into the International Tennis Hall of Fame in 1999, and he still competes regularly on the ATP Tour of Champions and other events.

But, if competing on the court is John's passion, it is by no means his only interest. He has achieved success as a network television commentator, author of a best-selling autobiography ("You Cannot Be Serious"), musician, philanthropist, and founder of The John McEnroe Tennis Academy in New York.

While his exploits have made "Mac" an international celebrity, to Kevin, Sean, Emily, Anna, Ava and Ruby he's still just "Dad". A concerned and loving parent and role model, John was the recipient of the 1996 National Father of the Year Award from the National Father's Day Council.

Foreword

By John McEnroe

Richmond, Virginia is one of the best tennis towns in America. Most importantly, it is the home of one of the greatest athletes and personalities our sport has ever known, the late, great Arthur Ashe.

Richmond has a great tradition of hosting professional tennis events. Some of my memories of playing in Richmond include losing to Bjorn Borg in the 1979 WCT tournament semifinal (after having 8 match points); playing with my brother Patrick to win the doubles title at the 1984 WCT tournament; returning to Richmond in 1985 to play my good friend and rival Bjorn Borg again in an exhibition match (I got my revenge and turned the tables on him!); playing against Jimmy Connors in a charity exhibition where we raised six figures for a local Richmond charity; playing doubles with my good friend from Richmond, Tommy Cain in a seniors tournament; and driving from New York to Richmond (shortly after the tragic 9/11 incident) to play in a 2001 Champions Tour event where I beat Mats Wilander in an emotionally charged event for all and then getting in my car again, immediately after the match, to drive home to see my family as soon as possible in New York City.

I applaud Richmond for its commitment to tennis and for bringing local tennis history back to life through this book.

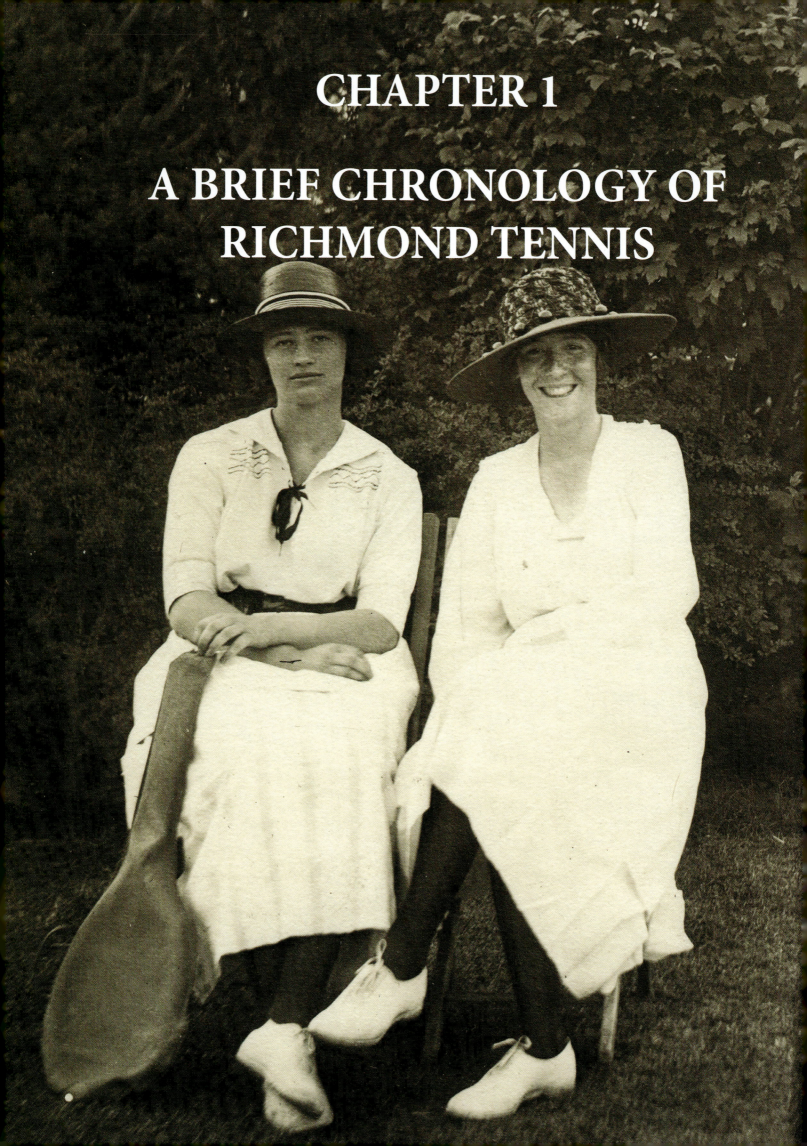

CHAPTER 1

A BRIEF CHRONOLOGY OF RICHMOND TENNIS

The Early Years of Tennis in Richmond

By Eric Perkins

The precise origin of tennis is the subject of much speculation and conjecture. In his definitive work, *The Bud Collins History of Tennis—An Authoritative Encyclopedia and Record Book*, the famed tennis writer and commentator suggests that the sport can trace its roots back to monks in the 12th century who began batting a ball back and forth to one another (and against the monastery walls) with their hands. Collins' research suggests that rackets did not become an added element to the game until perhaps as much as 400 years later.

Ladies Day on the dirt courts in the early 1900s. *Courtesy of Valentine Richmond History Center.*

Moving forward to the mid-1800s, the British patent office issued provisional letters of patent to Major Walter Wingfield for "A Portable Court of Playing Tennis" on February 23, 1874. Reports of this new game which offered great exercise for men, women, and children spread, and lawn tennis became increasingly popular as Wingfield's tennis equipment and rule book were sold all over the world[1].

The roots of tennis in Richmond can be traced back at least as far as the 1870s[2], when what is now downtown Richmond boasted no less than four tennis clubs, the largest of which was the Franklin Tennis Club, which had five dirt courts on West Franklin Street near Harrison Street for its 90 members (about one third of whom were women). In June 1892, the membership register

Opposite - Penelope Anderson and Elizabeth Warren won their first national girls doubles tournament in 1919. *Courtesy of Valentine Richmond History Center.*

---

[1] Collins, Bud. The Bud Collins History of Tennis. Canada: New Chapter Press. 2008.
[2] Henley, Bernard J. "The Early Years of Tennis in Richmond." The Richmond Literature and History Quarterly, Winter 1978.

of West-End Lawn Tennis Club included 24 men, and near the turn of the century, Hermitage Golf Club had three tennis courts.

The Island Club had two courts on Mayo Island, a privately owned, 13-acre island at the fall line of the James River in downtown Richmond. While club membership was open only to

Richmond's first mixed league team? This photo was taken around 1900 and you can see why the sport was generally referred to as lawn tennis in that era. *Courtesy of Valentine Richmond History Center.*

men, it was common for members to enjoy playing tennis for about an hour and then accompanying their lady friends on an afternoon sail on the James River. Island Club members had access to the boathouse at the Virginia Boat Club.

Two smaller tennis clubs during this era were the Casino Club on East Franklin near Second Street and the Richmond Club, which had only one court near the corner of Main and Foushee Streets.

Since there were no formal rankings or USTA-sanctioned tournaments, there was always a healthy debate as to who deserved bragging rights as the best player in town. One brave journalist in 1877 proclaimed Edith Donnan and Irene Pleasants as the area's top female tennis players and M.S. Triplett, Phillip Haxall, and Matthew Maury as the top men. The public debate continued, reflecting the sport's growing popularity and the passion for tennis found throughout the community.

The Country Club of Virginia ("CCV"), now with over 7,000 members and 24 indoor and outdoor courts, was first incorporated in 1908. As part of its initial membership campaign, a lifetime membership (no monthly dues…ever) was only $500, or, in 2012 dollars, the approximate equivalent of $12,000. Formed to offer tennis, golf, indoor games and amusements, horses, racetrack, skeet fields, boating, swimming pools, restaurant, and a bar, CCV had eight courts made of clay or crushed brick along the edge of St. Andrews Lane[3].

In the early 1900s, the members at Hermitage Country Club organized a major tournament called the "Old Dominion Tennis Tournament" which consistently drew nationally prominent players. The tournament moved in 1911 to CCV where it would be held until the end of its run in the 1930s—a casualty of the Great Depression. While Hermitage Country Club did a fair share of relocating over the years, tennis was always a part of its focus, and, ultimately, a separate tennis club, described by some as a club within a club, developed.

Another tennis highlight at CCV during this period was an array of challenge matches pitting a group of CCV men against collegiate teams. Early CCV losses to Harvard and Yale would be later offset by victories over UVA, Randolph-Macon College, and William and Mary, among others.

The 1930s saw the growth of professional tennis barnstorming tours across the country. Bill Tilden turned pro in 1931 to cash in on his fame. His troupe came to play at CCV several times during the 1930s, often drawing as many as 1,000 fans paying $1 per ticket.

In 1939, Richmond was the site of the first pro tennis tournament in Virginia. Joe Whalen of Memphis, Tennessee left town with the $100 top prize money in the 20-man tournament played at CCV.

The first Richmonder to make it big on the national tennis scene was Penelope "Nip" Anderson. As an eight-year-old in 1910, Penelope Anderson began playing tennis on a dirt court in a neighbor's backyard in Westhampton[4]. After honing her skills at CCV and first winning a national girls' doubles title in Philadelphia with her partner Elizabeth "Lib" Warren, in 1919, Anderson would later become the first Virginian to earn a national top ten ranking, reaching the quarterfinals at the U.S. Nationals on five separate occasions, recording victories over Grand Slam champions like Helen Jacobs, and representing the United States in Wightman Cup competition. The Anderson Cup, an annual interclub competition among CCV, Farmington Country Club in Charlottesville, Princess Anne Country Club in Virginia Beach, and the Norfolk Yacht and Country Club, is named after Penelope and her sister Margaret, who was also an avid and highly regarded tennis player.

During the pre-World War II era, top players in the area included Cliff Miller, who was city singles champion in 1930 and 1932-36, and Bobby Leitch, who won city singles championships in 1939-41 and again in 1946-47. Leitch captained the University of Richmond varsity tennis team, which posted a then-school best 19-1 record in 1937.

Harold "Hal" Burrows, Jr., who served as tennis director at CCV for 18 years, won multiple state titles as a junior from 1938-1942. Then, like many of the top male players of the era, took a hiatus from competitive tennis while serving in the armed forces. Upon returning home to Virginia, he quickly picked up where he left off, winning three consecutive Virginia State Men's Championships from 1946 to 1948 and enjoying a successful collegiate career playing on the men's varsity team at UVA. Burrows' success continued into the 1950s as a singles competitor and a member of a top-ten ranked doubles team with Straight Clark, reaching the latter rounds of Wimbledon and other major events around the world. Tennis trivia buffs will note that it was the team of Burrows and Clark that thwarted the Grand Slam bid of Lew Hoad and Ken Rosewall in 1953, winning a four-set battle at the U.S. Championships in Brookline, Massachusetts after the Aussies claimed doubles titles at the Australian Open, French Open, and Wimbledon that year. Burrows and Clark were named to the U.S. Davis Cup squad in 1954.

---

[3] Gibson, Jr., Lawrence. The Country Club of Virginia 1908-2008. Richmond, Virginia: The Country Club of Virginia, 2008.

[4] Simpson, William S. "Penelope Anderson: Virginia's Queen of Tennis." The Richmond Literature and History Quarterly, Winter 1979.

The Sam Woods Era (1940s-1950s)

By Eric Perkins

For many, the golden age of Richmond tennis began in 1943, when Sam Woods was asked to oversee junior tennis programming at Byrd Park. Woods, who left behind a successful insurance business and moved into a small shack at the Byrd Park tennis courts, would come to be known as "Mr. Tennis" for his tireless efforts to promote tennis at the public parks in an era where tennis was predominately limited to country clubs.

Woods made the most out of minimal resources and helped grow tennis at Byrd Park with his box of rackets and balls available for juniors who wanted to learn to play tennis. A small group of local supporters—the first Richmond tennis patrons—including Bobby Cabell, Sr., Cy Slavin, Al Dickinson and Bobby Leitch, helped raise funds to support Woods' tennis programs. In 1954, the Richmond Tennis Patrons Association (now known as the Richmond Tennis Association) was formally organized to support junior tennis development, primarily Woods' programs at Byrd Park.

Under Woods' leadership, Thomas Jefferson High School became a high school tennis dynasty in the late 1940s and 1950s, winning a string of 11 state championships, with many of those players earning scholarships to play tennis at college. Woods himself was an accomplished player, winning the Virginia State Doubles Championship during this period.

Woods also started running tournaments of all levels at Byrd Park. These events brought tremendous opportunities for local players to see and compete against top competition, and this exposure helped fuel the growth of junior tennis in Richmond for a generation. The Cavalier Invitational, one of Woods' early tournaments, drew nationally ranked players from across the eastern U.S. The tournament eventually came to be known as the Thalhimers Invitational and for many years was dominated by Woods' protégés. Gene Wash, Del Sylvia, Bobby Payne, and Bobby Bortner each won the tournament at least once during its successful run.

Sam Woods chats with two of his top students, Gene Wash (center) and Bobby Bortner (right) in 1951.

The Swingin' 60s

By Eric Perkins

Shortly after Sam Woods passed away in 1963, the tennis courts at Byrd Park were dedicated in his honor at a special ceremony. His memorial plaque still stands at the Sam Woods Memorial Courts at Byrd Park.

O.H. Parrish was widely regarded as one of Richmond's top players throughout the 1960s, winning state singles championships in 1963, '65, and '67 to go along with city titles in 1962, '65, '67, and '69. He was one of several Richmonders to play college tennis for UNC. As a Tar Heel, Parrish played on three ACC championship teams, winning the Atlantic Coast Conference championship at #1 singles in 1965 to go along with two conference doubles titles. When the ACC released its list of the top 50 ACC men's tennis players of all time in 2002, Parrish was on the list, as were fellow members of the Richmond-Tar Heel connection David Caldwell and Tripp Phillips.

John W. "Bitsy" Harrison, another UNC alum, was perhaps Richmond's top male player during the 1960s. Aside from winning the Richmond city title in 1960 and the Virginia state championship in 1966, Harrison was highly regarded at the national level as well, winning the prestigious Blue-Gray National Classic in 1965 (the VCU men's team claimed Blue-Gray team titles in 2003, 2004, and 2006). Harrison used his considerable height and power to be a formidable opponent at Grand Slam events, reaching the third round at the 1963 U.S. Open before losing to the legendary Roy Emerson. Nearly 50 years later, Emerson was the keynote speaker at the Richmond Tennis Hall of Fame Class of 2011 induction ceremony, and included in the Class of 2011 was none other than Bitsy Harrison.

Another top player from Richmond during the era was Tom Chewning, who practiced and played often with Arthur Ashe as a junior before heading to UNC for a successful collegiate career where he won three consecutive ACC singles titles at various positions from 1965 to 1967, following the high standards set by other Richmonders Parrish, Bruce Sylvia, and Bobby Bortner, all of whom claimed ACC singles titles for the Tar Heels.

On the women's side, Sarah Townsend was a dominant force on the local tournament circuit. She claimed four city titles (1962, '64, '65, and '68) and two state titles (1965-66). Sue Cain claimed the final city title of the decade, winning the women's singles title in 1969.

At the urging of Bill Riordan, famed tennis promoter and one-time manager of Jimmy Connors who had just started promoting the U.S. National Indoors in Salisbury, Maryland, the RTA and other tennis community leaders organized the area's first major indoor tournament in 1966. The Fidelity Bankers Life Invitational debuted at the Richmond Arena and was a staple of Richmond tennis (and primary fundraiser for the RTA) for nearly 20 years, concluding its successful run in 1984 as the United Virginia Bank Tennis Classic.

Through a series of meetings orchestrated by Massie Valentine, Ron Charity, and Lou Einwick, Arthur Ashe committed to return to Richmond as a main drawing card for the inaugural event in 1966. Arthur's homecoming was short lived, however. Big-serving Frank Froehling took advantage of the fast canvas court and upset Ashe in the opening round. Noticeably struggling to follow his opponent's blistering serves, Ashe, who suffered from recurrent eye inflammations, went to an optometrist immediately after the tournament and was fitted with glasses.

Westwood built the first indoor courts in Richmond, a four-court structure completed in 1966, and was among the first tennis clubs to hire a full-time teaching pro. CCV, Willow Oaks and Hermitage Country Club had resident pros at the time, but indoor courts would follow years later as they and other clubs followed Westwood's lead truly making tennis a year-round sport in Richmond. Starting in 1967, a professional women's invitational event at Westwood brought top players like Maria Bueno, Nancy Richey, and Peaches Barkowicz to town.

Announced at the time as the "most significant tennis event in state history," Richmond hosted its first U.S. Davis Cup tie in May 1968. It is more than ironic that Arthur Ashe led the U.S. team to victory over a thoroughly outmatched British Caribbean squad at Byrd Park—the same public court facility where he was turned away as a young child in the unfortunate era of segregation.

In September 1968, Ashe won the U.S. Open (as an amateur, he collected a mere $20 per day in expense money—far below the $1.8 million Novak Djokovic took home after winning the 2011 U.S. Open) and was on his way to becoming the number one-ranked player in the world in 1969. The fact that the Ashe-led U.S. team was still in contention for the Davis Cup was the only reason he had not yet been ordered to return to military duty as a computer programming instructor at the U.S. Military Academy at West Point, New York.

Ashe co-founded the National Junior Tennis League ("NJTL") in 1969 as a national network of organizations dedicated to promoting character development of youth through tennis, with an emphasis on the values of humanitarianism, leadership, and academic excellence. Richmond had one of the first NJTL chapters (there are currently four NJTL chapters in the area), and by the early 70s, Richmond Parks and Recreation's NJTL chapter had over 1,300 kids participating.

Richmond Tennis Hall of Famer Rodney Harmon was first introduced to tennis at Battery Park through Richmond's NJTL program. "Richmond had 6-8 teams in its NJTL program at the time," Harmon recalls, "University of Richmond student Colin Gibb was our team captain, and while I was too young to play on the team that year, I remember that my team won nationals." NJTL was huge in Richmond at that time. Harmon notes that other top players like Junie Chatman and Rozzell Lightfoot also came out of the NJTL program.

The NJTL organization grew into a national organization providing tennis, education, and life skills instruction to over 250,000 children through 600+ local chapters by 2011. Notably, one of our local NJTL chapters, Lobs & Lessons, was announced as a national chapter of the year award winner in January 2012 at the USTA's Community Tennis Development Workshop in New Orleans.

The idea of the Richmond Suburban Ladies Tennis League was first conceived in 1964 when the Recreation Association Tennis League began as a men's summer league. By 1968, plans were formally put into action when a group of ladies decided to form a "social tennis league" similar to the men's league. A League Constitution was drafted with the following purpose of fostering "friendly tennis competition among the member groups." The charter clubs were Southampton, Avalon, Bon Air, Canterbury, Chamberlayne, Chestnut Oaks, CCV, Kanawha, Mechanicsville, Ridgetop, Three Chopt, Westwood, and Willow Oaks.

League Bylaws allowed a maximum of 20 clubs, and by 1993 Brandermill, Briarwood, Burkwood, Raintree, Hermitage, Richmond Country Club, Salisbury, and Stonehenge had been admitted to the league. The structure of the league and its format was strategically planned--league matches were designed to begin at 9:30 am and consist of four eight-game pro set singles and three ten-game pro set doubles matches so that stay-at-home mothers could send their children off to school, play tennis, and arrive home before their children. The league was designed to have three levels, A, B, and C. The A-level included the top teams as well as the top team which consisted of "championship" level players. There was also a "fun level" for beginners. However, most teams were formed based on friendships, not talent recruiting efforts.

The league has steadily grown and evolved over the years. After a Bylaw amendment opened the league to more clubs, Woodlake was admitted into the league in 1995 after being on the waiting list for 20 years. In 2012, over 2,500 women participate in the league, representing 31 local clubs. There are still A, B, and C levels, but the championship teams have become a fourth level of their own. As further proof of the passion Richmond has for tennis, the league to this day is managed exclusively by volunteers, with chairmanship rotating among the member clubs.

Another organization that would quickly become an institution of Richmond junior tennis—the Richmond Junior Suburban Tennis League ("RJSTL")—debuted in 1969 under the leadership of Lila Williamson Gilliam and support from a vast team of parent volunteers and local clubs. Recognizing that there was a vastly underserved market of juniors throughout the community with the desire and talent to play tennis (juniors who were flying under the radar of the RTA), Gilliam led a monumental effort to create a city-wide junior tennis league. From its bootstrapping beginnings, the league reached its peak in 1977 when it had over 900 participants from 18 local clubs and neighborhood associations, including Avalon, Bon Air, Briarwood, Canterbury, Chamberlayne, Chestnut Oaks, CCV, Kanawha, Lakeside, Raintree, Ridgetop, Salisbury, Southhampton, Surreywood, Three Chopt, Westwood, Willow Oaks, and Woodmont. The strength of the RJSTL and its enduring success more than 40 years later can be traced to the loyal support of the volunteer team captains and club representatives who coordinate all aspects of the league—a wonderful example of our city's passion for tennis and devotion to family and community.

The RTA junior development program was where the area's top juniors and instructors congregated to train. Whether at the Field House at St. Christopher's School or at Westwood, the high level of competition and sense of camaraderie was a key factor in continuing the tradition started by Sam Woods at Byrd Park. This program produced nationally prominent juniors for several decades.

The Booming 70s

By Eric Perkins

Nowhere in the nation was the tennis "boom" of the 1970s more forcefully felt than in Richmond. With an active community tennis association, successful pro tournaments, increasing numbers of players clogging tennis courts all over town, private club expansion, tennis shops providing all the latest in tennis fashions, equipment, and supplies, Richmond was abuzz with tennis fever.

Wayne Tucker, Gene Freund, and Dick Shockley opened the area's first retail tennis shop, generating a reported $250,000 in sales in 1974, the year Jimmy Connors and Chris Evert were dominating the professional tennis world. A new Arthur Ashe fiberglass and aluminum racket was priced at $50 and a pair of tennis shoes would set you back $33. The shop also advertised tennis gloves (in a variety of colors!) for only $5.

Local teaching pro Fred Koechlein became the tennis director at the new Virginia All-Weather Tennis facility on Parham Road. The 4-court indoor facility offered a 29-week winter tennis season with court capacity filled over 85% of the time between 8:00 am and 11:00 pm 7 days a week. This was symbolic of the growth and development of indoor tennis where "pay-for-play" practices were no obstacle to filling indoor courts.

Tennis in Richmond outgrew the country clubs during this period. Tennis courts became a standard feature along with swimming pools at apartment communities built during the 70s. Local tennis tournament draws began to grow dramatically. Tennis activity at public parks grew to unprecedented levels. On any given sunny weekend at Byrd Park, players knew to expect a wait of anywhere from one to three hours for a court. At its peak, the city of Richmond's summer tennis program grew to 30 summer employees serving 2,000 kids.

It was also during this period that the first calls for a large indoor community tennis center came from the public—perhaps as many as 25 to 32 indoor and outdoor courts and a permanent staff to conduct year-round programming. Such calls have remained consistent throughout the decades and today. Imagine what a world-class community tennis center would offer not only to the tennis community, but the entire metropolitan community!

In the fall of 1970, a group of professional tennis ladies known as the "Original Nine" played in a historical tournament at Westwood. This distinguished group of players, Billie Jean King, Kristy Pigeon, Val Ziegenfuss, Nancy Richey, Stephanie Johnson, Mary Ann Curtis, Denise Carter, Rosie Casals, Darlene Hard and Ceci Martinez just weeks before had announced the launch of the first all-women's tennis event known as the "Virginia Slims Invitational Tour." It turned out that Westwood hosted the second event of the fledgling tour, with Billie Jean King winning her first Virginia Slims tour title. In 1971, Billie Jean became the first female athlete to earn $100,000 in one year and the women's professional tour grew to a multi-million dollar enterprise featuring events all over the world. Westwood hosted two more Virginia Slims tour events in 1972 and 1973.

By summer 1974, Raintree joined the ranks of leading tennis clubs in the area. Initiation fees ranged from $400 to $1,300, with monthly dues ranging from $30 to $40. Other indoor tennis clubs emerged throughout the decade. Courtside West opened in 1978 to offer yet another indoor tennis alternative for players in Richmond's far West End, and Courtside South (also known as Courtside Brandermill) opened soon thereafter in Midlothian.

A brief review of the 1974 Middle Atlantic Lawn Tennis Association (now known as the USTA/Mid-Atlantic Section) rankings reflect the dominance of Richmond in the world of junior tennis during the 70s. Ranked at or near the top of the sectional rankings were:

Tom Magner-Neal Carl (#7 men's doubles)
Tony Velo (#3 boys 18s)
Tommy Cain (#2 boys 16s)
Bobby Fauntleroy (#7 singles boys 16s,
   #1 boys 16s doubles with David Hawkins)
Jimmy Cain (#5 boys 14s)
Robert Menuet (#10 boys 14s)
Chris Conquest (#5 boys 12s)
Martha Beddingfield (#4 girls 18s)
Ann Grubbs (#8 girls 18s)
Becky Nierle (#10 girls 18s)

Betty Harrison (# 7 women's singles)
Brad Baylor (#7 boys 18s)
David Hawkins (#4 boys 16s)
Brian Gager (# 8 boys 16s)
Rodney Harmon (#1 boys 14s)
Butch Butcher (#9 boys 14s)
Greg Miller (#2 boys 12s)
Hal Greer (#7 boys 12s)
Heidi Markel (#6 girls 18s)
Karen Williams (#9 girls 18s)
Lloyd Hatcher (#1 girls 16s).

One of the RTA's key programs supporting the development of the area's most promising juniors has been its junior travel committee. Chaired by dedicated volunteers like Gayle St. Clair, the committee would select a handful of deserving juniors for sponsorship to cover the costs of traveling to play in major national tournaments. One issue of World Tennis magazine reportedly recognized Richmond for having more juniors with top 10 national rankings that any other metro area in the nation. Among the many stellar accomplishments, Leanne Seward was among the area's best juniors breaking into the U.S. top 10 in the 14-under division in 1978.

Locally, tournament tennis thrived during this period. The city tournament, sponsored by Thalhimers (a popular department store in the Richmond area until 1992), routinely had over a thousand participants in nearly two dozen different age divisions. The Home Beneficial Life Insurance Company was title sponsor of a popular and prestigious junior tournament held during the summer. Directed by JoAnne and John LeVay during its heyday, the tournament attracted over 400 juniors from across the Mid-Atlantic Section. During its prime, the Sam Woods Memorial Junior Tournament, under the leadership of Hugh Waters and John McGinty, drew more than 500 participants.

Richmond's finest teamed up for the 1975 Hotchkiss Cup competition.
Standing from left: Paul Dickinson, Mark Vines, O. H. Parrish, John Leitch, Tommy Cain, Rob Leitch, Chris Blair and Neal Carl. Kneeling: Tom Magner.
Courtesy of Richmond Times-Dispatch.

For adults, the RTA offered the Greater Richmond Adult Novice Tournament for several years under the direction of Ward Hamilton.

Dominant players on the local tournament circuit during the decade included:

Tommy Cain, who won back-to-back city titles as a teenager in 1976-1977 while excelling on the national junior tournament circuit. Cain went on play varsity tennis at Southern Methodist University and several years on the pro tour. Professional highlights included a win over then-world No. 4 Johan Kriek and a spectacular match against former world No. 1 Guillermo Vilas at the 1983 U.S. Open, where Cain extended the 1977 U.S. and French Open champion to five sets before losing.

Mark Vines, who won three city titles over a 15-year span (1975, '87, and '90) to go along with his four state titles (1977, '81, '87, and '89). Vines also was a nationally prominent junior who played for SMU in college and had a successful stint on the pro tour in the early 80s, including an ATP tournament victory at the 1981 Paris Masters. Vines continues to compete in age division events, holding top rankings in various age divisions and winning the 2012 ITF Men's 55s World Singles Championship.

Tom Magner, three-time city champion (1973, '74, and '79) and one of the area's top teaching pros since the early 70s at local clubs including Raintree and Jefferson-Lakeside.

Junie Chatman, two-time city champion (1978 and '83) and state champion in 1983, was another nationally prominent junior who played tennis for UNC, where he won three-straight ACC singles titles at various positions from 1976-1978, before venturing onto the pro tour for several years.

Mark Vines and Junie Chatman were among several Richmonders to compete on the pro tour in the 1980s. *Courtesy of Richmond Times-Disptach.*

Kathleen Cummings, Richmond's premier female junior competitor during the 1970s and youngest-ever winner of the women's city title in 1976-1977. Cummings also won the state singles title in 1979 and broke into the top 50 on the pro tour, competing at Wimbledon and other pro tournaments (including an upset win over 1977 Wimbledon champion Virginia Wade). She earned a scholarship to play for University of Colorado where she was an All-American for three years before transferring to University of Texas for her senior year, leading the Longhorn women's team to the Southwest Conference team title in 1984 while earning a top 5 national ranking and Conference Player of the Year honors, among many other accolades.

Kathleen Cummings, a two-time winner of the women's city tennis championship and member of the Richmond Tennis Hall of Fame. *Courtesy of Richmond Times-Dispatch.*

Rodney Harmon, a product of local NJTL and RTA programs, was a nationally prominent junior during the 70s, earning a tennis scholarship to play at Southern Methodist University. He was a three-time All-American before finishing his college career at the University of Tennessee, where he won the NCAA doubles championship with Mel Purcell. Rodney broke into the top 60 on the pro tour in the early 80s, topped by a Cinderella run to the quarterfinals of the 1982 U.S. Open, losing to eventual champion Jimmy Connors. After retiring from the pro tour, he held several high-profile positions with the USTA, including Director of Men's Tennis for USTA High Performance and coach of the U.S. Olympic tennis team in 2008. He also coached the men's tennis team at the University of Miami and is currently tennis director at one of Florida's most prestigious tennis clubs.

The Harmon brothers - Rodney (right) and Marell (left) - led a high-powered boys team at Thomas Jefferson High School in the mid 70s. *Courtesy of Richmond Times-Dispatch.*

Barring injury or major scheduling conflicts, the area's top players could always be counted on to compete in the Thalhimers city tournament. The men's draw, in particular, would often attract more than 150 entrants, requiring some players to play in a qualifying tournament to earn a spot in the main draw. The competition was fierce and the drama could be spine-tingling, such as the 1977 quarterfinal match between #8 Ward Hamilton and top-seeded Mark Vines. Hamilton, a highly regarded player and teaching pro at the Richmond Tennis Academy, recorded one of the more dramatic wins and biggest upsets in city tournament history by serving an ace on double match point at 4-4 in the "sudden death" nine-point tiebreaker to win 6-3, 0-6, 7-6 (5-4).

On the women's side, repetition was the theme for the decade as an elite group were repeat winners of the singles title: Lindsay Burn (1970 - 1971), Flo Bryan (1972 - 1974), Kathleen Cummings (1976 - 1977) and Leanne Seward (1978 - 1980).

In August 1975, Richmond fielded a team for the National Girls City Team matches in Bowie, Maryland. Representing Richmond were Lloyd Hatcher, Betty Baugh Harrison, Martha Beddingfield, Ann Grubbs, Kathleen Cummings and Heidi Markel.

Hugh Waters and Ward Hamilton opened the Richmond Tennis Academy in a converted warehouse in Richmond's West End, producing literally hundreds of tournament caliber juniors in an environment that promoted tennis, fun, and hard work. Juniors would stay all day drilling and playing matches. The low ceilings forced players to concentrate extra hard on their shot selection and mental toughness. Gary Wilmot and Bill Doeg were the head pros at the academy, along with Waters and Hamilton.

In 1977, the RTA helped organize the Life of Virginia Junior Invitational Tennis Tournament, hosting the nation's top juniors in the 16s and 18s. Directed by Jerry DePew, this tournament exposed local players to top competition and helped boost the level of junior play in our community. Some of the notable participants in the event during its four-year run include future world top ten players Andrea Jaeger, Jimmy Arias, and Tim Mayotte. Proving that Richmonders can compete with the nation's elite, seeded players at the 1979 event included: Jeff Jones, Chris Conquest, Steve Wilson, Damian Sancilio, Darryl Wilburn and David Wolfe on the boys' side and Margie Waters, Sandra Beddingfield, Kathleen Cummings, Leanne Seward, and Stacy Moss on the girls' side. Rodney Harmon won the boys 18s title in front of his hometown fans in 1979.

Sue Cain was a fixture on the tennis scene during this period, serving terms as President of the RTA, Greater Richmond Tennis Umpires Association (GRTUA), and USTA/Virginia while continuing to be an active tennis player (1969 city champion), tennis parent, and a pioneer as a female tennis official.

Sue Cain began the Richmond Umpires Association and went on to umpire at Wimbledon, Australian Open, Seoul Olympics and U.S. Open, where she officiated the final between Chris Evert and Martina Navratilova.

Numerous special events and promotions over the years have taken tennis to the streets in downtown Richmond. *Courtesy of Richmond Times-Dispatch*.

The Roaring 80s

By Eric Perkins

The USTA created a national league program in 1980—with competition beginning at local levels and top teams advancing through district, sectional, and national championships—and Richmond tennis would never be the same. Providing opportunities for fun and competitive play, the USTA League concept was embraced by the Richmond tennis community. With Michelob Light as title sponsor, guidance from sectional and district staff, support from local clubs, and efficient leadership from a small network of local league coordinators, the USTA League grew from 13,000 participants in its debut year to its current tally of well over half a million participants across the country.

Richmond's first foray into the USTA League program started with a 5.0 league in 1982 coordinated by Terry Frazier and Hugh Waters. Tom Magner came to Briarwood in 1983 and rated many players (remember those rating clinics conducted under the watchful eyes of certified NTRP verifiers who evaluated players and assigned NTRP ratings?) to kickstart leagues at 3.5 and 4.5 levels with about four teams in each league. In the late 80s, Alan Harrell and P.J. Mahoney took over local league administration and assigned coordinators to run a full slate of 3.0, 3.5, 4.0, 4.5 and 5.0 leagues. Mahoney was just as active as a league player. Eleven of his Senior and Super Senior teams have made it to nationals.

The USTA certainly did not have a monopoly on league tennis in Richmond. The Richmond Suburban Ladies League, the Saturday morning "Racket League," and the Richmond Junior Suburban ("Bantam") Leagues, among others, continued to thrive.

Rozzell Lightfoot took advantage of all the bustling tennis activity at Battery Park to become a top contender on the local junior tournament circuit in the 80s, veteran of the ATP Tour and now director of a tennis academy in the DC area. *Courtesy of Richmond Times-Dispatch.*

The University of Richmond women's team led by Martha Beddingfield and Sharon Dunsing won the AIAW Division II national championship in 1982.

Another one of Richmond's top players, Damian Sancilio, was one of a select handful of players who won city titles both as a junior and as an adult—claiming junior titles in the 16s and 18s divisions in the early 80s and adding titles in the men's open division in 1984 and 2007. After a successful collegiate career at UVA, Sancilio worked several years as a tennis coach for the Kuwaiti national team before returning to Richmond, where he is now both a club owner and top teaching pro.

Top juniors coming up through the RTA junior program and earning top state and sectional rankings throughout the 1980s and into the 90s included: (boys) Mark Arrowsmith, Bruce Bigger, Ian Boettcher, David Caldwell, Paul Caldwell, John Chichester, Sonny Dearth, Erik DeVries, Sears Driscoll, Cole Durrill, Charles Einwick, Daniel Grinnan, Landon Harper, Joey Hopke, Matt Hopke, John Hudson, Kevin Long, Matt Magner, Wade McGuire, Travis Miller, Chris Mumford, Keith Mumford, Tripp Phillips, Cris Robinson, Jim Thompson, Charles

Valentine, Chris Wallace; (girls) Shawn Arrowsmith, Katherine Chen, Shannon Cubitt, Valerie Farmer, Stephanie Hiedemann, Tricia Holder, Jamie Marlowe, Melissa Mason, Dabney Mercer, Tinsley Mercer, Kimberly Nance, Christy Pomeroy, Tami Riehm, Christen Worthington and Jane Wright.

The 1988 Midlothian High School girls tennis team featured some of the area's top juniors. Seated from left: Wendy Perna, Tami Riehm, Jean Blutenthel, Missy Roberts, Kimberly Nance, Karen Schwartz, Shannon Cubitt and Becky Henry. *Courtesy of Richmond Times-Dispatch.*

Junie Chatman returned to Richmond after a stint on the pro tour to teach tennis at Briarwood for several years and then as director of tennis programming for the City of Richmond. His leadership boosted the energy and enthusiasm at public tennis courts around town, as evident by the sheer numbers of players that continued to fill the courts and tournament draws throughout the decade. In 1983 he became the first African-American male to win the Virginia State Tennis Championships at Raintree, defeating Mark Vines 6-3, 6-0 in the men's singles final.

Ed and Lynda Smith opened Plaid Racquet in the Gayton Crossing Shopping Center in 1989. It remains the premier tennis shop in the area.

The Soaring 90s

By Eric Perkins

Tennis in Richmond continued to flourish on all fronts during the 90s, cranking out top juniors who excelled on a national level. Topping the list during the late 80s and into the 90s were David Caldwell, Wade McGuire and Cris Robinson, all of whom were All-Americans at premier NCAA Division I tennis programs (UNC, Georgia, and Clemson, respectively). Caldwell ended his junior career in style—as the nation's #1 ranked player in the boys 18s. He continued that momentum at UNC where he was a two-time All-American, three-time ACC Player of the Year and made it to the quarters at the 1995 NCAA tournament. Always known for his sportsmanship, he once became so distraught during a match at a junior sectional championship that he had possibly missed a call, he actually asked an official to default him during the next changeover. The official politely refused, and although the mental lapse did cost him the first set, Caldwell regrouped to win the match and the tournament.

David Caldwell finished his junior career ranked No. 1 in the nation in the Boys 18s.

Wade McGuire was one of Richmond's top juniors. Coached for several years by Brandermill teaching pro John DePew, himself a top junior in the 70s, the thin, redheaded McGuire was a national junior star, state high school singles champion at Mills Godwin in 1987 and became the youngest men's city champion in 1986 (beating Tommy Cain's record by a few months). He was runner-up at the NCAA tournament in both 1992 and 1993 before turning pro and spending the rest of the decade traveling the world competing on the ATP Tour.

Cris Robinson's competitive career saw him go from competing in the 10s at Battery Park in the Southeastern Open to winning no less than five national amateur championships by the early 90s, with a #2 national ranking to go along with a state clay court championship and many other tournament victories. He was a star player at Clemson University, being named to the All-ACC team and selected as his team's MVP in 1994-95. One of his biggest victories was a 2003 win over rising star and current world top 10 John Isner at the CVITT tournament in Lynchburg. After college, Robinson returned to Richmond to become one of the area's top teaching pros and tennis innovators.

Chris Mumford was another Richmond native who grew up in a tennis family and excelled on the junior tournament circuit. As a senior at St. Christopher's, he won both singles and doubles titles at the High School National Interscholastics. Mumford earned both All-ACC and All-American honors at UNC and, among his many notable tournament wins, he won the Virginia State Clay Court title in 1991, defeating Virginia Tech standout Jon Ramthun in the final.

On the women's side, former William and Mary star Julie Kaczmarek Ogborne and Rachel Gale were generally regarded as the top female players in Richmond, both winning titles in singles, doubles, and mixed doubles at major tournaments in the area and also competing at national and international events with great success. Ogborne has become the architect of many great tournaments and events at CCV, where she has worked for nearly twenty years. Gale has taught tennis at various clubs throughout the area and served a stint as coach of the women's team at Meredith College in North Carolina before recently returning to Richmond as a director of junior tennis at ACAC in Midlothian.

In 1994, Ian Boettcher was ranked No. 1 in the Mid-Atlantic Section boys 16s, and yet he struggled to reach the top spot on his high school team because Mills Godwin was loaded that year with a trio of Bosnian exchange students sponsored by the RTA and hosted by community tennis supporters like the Lodens and the Thornes.

Byrd Park was site of the American Tennis Association National Championships in 1993 and 1994, under the direction of the local ATA chapter, the Capital City Tennis Club.

Brandermill hosted the 1993 National Intercollegiate Clay Court Championships, which featured Wade McGuire as the top seed.

Meanwhile, 13-year-old Mandy Pallais won a 1998 USTA/Mid-Atlantic Section Girls 18s Championship beating Midlothian's Kristin Lanio in the final and ending the year ranked #11 in the nation in the girls 14s. Rather than pursue a career in tennis, however, Pallais would go on to earn a Ph.D. in Economics at M.I.T. and become a faculty member at Harvard University.

Monacan High School star Joey Hopke won the 1997 Virginia State High School AAA singles crown by defeating Douglas Freeman's Jay Bruner 6-3, 7-6 in the final. He then teamed with his brother Matt to win the doubles title.

Marshall and Eddie Parker acquired Raintree Swim and Racquet Club in 1998 and continued to add to Raintree's great legacy in the tennis community through its strong junior development program and commitment to hosting the Virginia State Tennis Championships and a long list of junior tournaments and special events.

As described in more detail later in the book, the "Jimmy Connors" senior tour had a successful run in Richmond from 1997-2001 at Robious, Hermitage, and finally at the Siegel Center. A number of local players, including Chris Conquest, Greg Williams, Paul Caldwell, Sr., Robert Hetherington, Larry Rauppius, Fred McGlynn, Chris Blair, Jim Shakespeare, among others, continued to play regularly at sectional and national tournaments in their respective age divisions.

Cris Robinson, pictured with his collection of gold and silver balls for first and second place showings at USTA national championships.

Richmond 4.5 men's team that won the 2001 USTA League National Championship in Tucson, AZ (bottom row from left) Eric Perkins, John Hudson, Bill Barnes (Captain), John DePew and Will Kaufman; (top row from left) Bob Maddox, Tom Bailey (Asst. Captain), Tom Ager, Joe Cole and Brian Clark.

LOCAL TEAMS THAT WON USTA LEAGUE NATIONAL CHAMPIONSHIPS

1993 - MEN'S 4.5 TEAM. BILL BARNES, PONCHO BOWLING, STEVE GOAD, RANDY JONES, REGGIE KRUSZEWSKI, JERRY RAMSEY, KEN RIEHM, JIM ROBERTSON, SAVVA ROUBANIS AND RICKY ROWE

1997 - MEN'S 4.0 TEAM. JOHN BUTLER, DAVID CARTER, JOE DROTER, JEFF HANNER, TED LUSE, RONNIE MILLIGAN, BART NELSON, TAD TIERNEY AND WALTER WYATT

2000 - MEN'S 4.5 TEAM. BILL BARNES, TOM BAILEY, JOE COLE, GLENN HUGHES, KEVIN LONG, AL STRICKLER, FRED MCGLYNN, BILL CARLI, BRIAN CLARK, TRAVIS MILLER AND CHRIS WALLACE

2001 - MEN'S 4.5 TEAM. BILL BARNES, TOM BAILEY, JOE COLE, TOM AGER, BRIAN CLARK, JOHN DEPEW, JOHN HUDSON, WILL KAUFMAN, BOB MADDOX AND ERIC PERKINS

2002 - SENIOR MEN'S 4.0 TEAM. P.J. MAHONEY, PANCHO BOWLING, JOHN BRITTON, WILLIAM DALY, CRAIK GOODSPEED, REGGIE KRUSZEWSKI, JOHN LANIER, JAMES ROBERTSON AND WAYNE WATKINS

The 21st Century

By Eric Perkins

A group of local pros including Eddie Parker, Julie Ogborne, Cris Robinson, Scott Steinour, Mark Bernstine, and Joe Cappellino formed the Association of Richmond Tennis Professionals in October 2001 as a charitable vehicle to promote an innovative series of one-day, alternative format junior tournaments for juniors who were new to competitive tennis. The summer series of tournaments steadily grew to over 900 participants and featured an end-of-season Masters event at CCV.

On the men's side, the defining rivalry of the period was Sean Steinour versus Carl Clark. Both men came to Richmond in the mid 90s to spearhead tennis programs at Westwood and CCV, respectively, and they quickly established themselves as the men to beat on the local tournament circuit, exchanging victories at many of the major tournaments in the area.

But at the turn of the century, it was the brother-sister tandem of Jay and Bridget Bruner who were stealing the show, with impressive back-to-back victories at the Davenport City Tournament in 2000-2001 (a feat not seen since Damian and Diane Sancilio won men's and women's city titles in 1984), followed by victories at the Virginia State Tennis Championships at Raintree. Hailing from an award-winning tennis family, both had successful junior careers and continue to be active in the tennis community to this day, with Jay as coach of the men's tennis program at College of Charleston and Bridget as a local teaching pro and Director of Administration for the RTA.

Top area juniors participating in RTA junior development programs and competing at sectional and national events in the early 2000s included Ryan Mostrom, Randy Loden, Bo Young, Lindsey Howard, Kate Harrington, Cathy Nimitz (followed closely by her younger sister Kristin), Britt Aspinall and Koren Fleming.

One of the more memorable stories from the 2002 tournament season was Melissa Robinson's inspiring run to the women's singles title at the Virginia State Clay Court Championships, where she beat Julie Ogborne, Rachel Gale, and Lindsey Wyeth in succession to win the crown.

McDonald's signed on to replace the Richmond Times-Dispatch as the new title sponsor for the RTA's summer junior tournament series in 2003, joining Anthem and Davenport and Company as key corporate sponsors of RTA events.

The RTA formally entered the social media revolution with the debut of its website www.richmondtennis.org in 2005. The organization received great publicity thanks to a Comcast "Local Edition" feature that aired for several weeks during the winter

Bridget Reichert (left) and Ginny Wortham, finalists of the 2011 city tournament.

of 2005-2006, serving as a local reminder of the bustling tennis activity taking place on a year-round basis in Richmond.

Throughout the decade, the RTA sponsored a winter indoor program at Raintree, Westwood and Robious providing low cost training opportunities for over 100 local juniors, as well as periodic high school coaches clinics and a summer junior program coordinated by Paul Manning at local public parks in partnership with various community groups like the City of Richmond, U-Turn, Police Athletic League, and the new Metro Richmond Tennis Club.

A new organization called Tennis for Life was started by a group of tennis parents and teaching pros, such as Pat Anderson and Jamie Morgan, to provide more focused and intensive training for some of the area's top junior talent.

In 2006, the clay court tournament at Salisbury Country Club was promoted from a state-level clay court championship to being sanctioned as the USTA/Mid-Atlantic Section's Clay Court Championship. Coupled with an increasing pool of prize money and a growing number of corporate sponsors, Bill Barnes and Scott Steinour continued to build the tournament into one of the finest in the Mid-Atlantic region that now regularly draws top collegiate and pro circuit players from all over the country.

(l to r) Brenda Schultz-McCarthy, Katrina Adams, Luke Jensen and Rodney Harmon were the featured celebrity pros at a fundraising Pro-Am at Willow Oaks sponsored by the Virginia Tennis Foundation in March 2011.

The Recreation Association Challenge debuted in October 2007. Under the leadership of Rob Johnston and Charlie Palmer and with assistance from the RTA, the Anthem Challenge spin-off featured a weekend competition with teams from Avalon, Ridgetop, Kanawha, Bon Air, Canterbury and Richmond Country Club participating over the years. Now known as the Autumn Cup, the event continues to grow.

Wheelchair tennis in Richmond has gained a lot of attention in recent years thanks to new programs and the area's first USTA-sanctioned wheelchair tennis tournament at Midlothian Athletic Club. Led by volunteer leaders Joe and Shima Grover, in 2007 the RTA began a relationship with Sportable, a local adaptive sports organization, to support and promote wheelchair tennis in the community. This effort has blossomed into a year-round wheelchair tennis program at Byrd Park and other activities throughout the year.

The Bon Air 4.0 women's team concluded the 2011 season with a second place finish at the USTA League National Championships.

At the end of 2007, Lou Einwick stepped down as Executive Director of the RTA, following nearly five decades of distinguished service to the organization. To many in Richmond, the name Lou Einwick was synonymous with the RTA. A reception in his honor took place at Westwood, featuring remarks from Donald Dell and other dignitaries from the tennis community. Lest anyone thought Einwick would disappear from the tennis scene, he continues to be instrumental in various RTA projects, most notably the RTA's annual "Dream

Weekend at the U.S. Open" raffle that raised over $50,000 during its five-year run from 2007-2011. The RTA named the men's city singles championship trophy the Einwick Cup in his honor.

The women's city singles championship trophy was named the Wortham Cup in honor of former city champion and longtime tennis supporter Lindsay Burn Wortham. It is only fitting that Lindsay's daughter Ginny was the first player to raise the Wortham Cup in victory as she won back-to-back city titles in 2009 and 2010.

Carl Clark emerged with the Davenport city singles title in 2008 with a series of victories over several champions of tomorrow (12-year old Shyam Venkatasubramanian and teenager Kyle Parker) before beating eight-time city champion Sean Steinour in the final. The 2008 city tournament also saw the return of Tom Cain who, following a 31-year absence from the tournament, teamed with Clark to win the men's doubles crown.

The "Battle of the Pros" debuted in May 2008 as a fun event showcasing the area's top teaching pros and juniors in a team-format competition.

Newcomers Romain Ambert, Michal Ciszek, and Martin Stiegwardt were dominant forces on the local tournament circuit from 2006-2010. Ambert, a two-time All-American at Mississippi State and currently Director of Junior Tennis at Westwood, won four consecutive Virginia State Indoor titles at CCV from 2006-2009.

Stiegwardt, a national champion in his native Ecuador and member of Ecuador's 2002 Davis Cup team, won the 2009 city championship defeating both Sean Steinour and Carl Clark in straight sets for the singles title. He was a teaching pro at Willow Oaks Country Club for several years and is currently an assistant coach for the VCU tennis team.

The 2011 Battle of the Pros brought out Richmond's best players, including (from left) Julie Ogborne, Romain Ambert, Lynn Bybee, Jamie Hevron, Max Schnur, Trip Baisden, Eddie Parker and Sofia Hiort-Wright.

Ciszek also arrived in Richmond with an impressive resume, including ATP tour and Davis Cup experience, and made his mark by winning the area's two most prestigious tournaments in 2010, beating David Shay 6-3, 6-2 to win the Davenport city title on the hard courts at Byrd Park in May and then winning the McDonald's Mid-Atlantic Clay Court title in July with a tough 6-4, 7-6 victory over UVA star Sanam Singh in the final. Ciszek currently is a teaching pro at Willow Oaks Country Club.

Tragedy struck the tennis community in December 2009 when Keith Mumford, a life-long competitive tennis player, volunteer and former RTA board member, suffered a massive heart attack while playing tennis one December evening at Westwood. With the support of family and friends, Keith heroically fought

Chris Mumford and Sears Driscoll, winners of the inaugural Keith Mumford Memorial Doubles Tournament at CCV in June 2010.

To Him, Tennis Was A Love Game

Keith Mumford was a little bit of all of us but stronger than most, an ordinary guy who showed extraordinary character and determination to make the most of what he was given in life. Beginning with childhood Hodgkin's cancer at the age of 13, to the massive heart attack at the age of 40, through his six-month struggle to survive, he was a man of courage. He was a youth tournament player who was always good for a couple of rounds, but not often the finals. Still he persisted. A high school player who gave his St. Christopher's School team the depth to literally dominate the Prep League in the mid-80s, he was an unlikely walk-on at Vanderbilt who gave that team an extra measure of character, determination, and love for each other that lives on today. Keith was a club player, who in recent years could compete with anyone. As a young man, Keith worked in the pro shops at Raintree and Briarwood and taught tennis at Briarwood, at Salisbury, for the RTPA (now the RTA), and on the streets of New York. He was successful everywhere not because he had incredible ability, but because he had developed a special grace and purity in his tennis strokes and his relationships. His wonderful spirit lives on through all of us who knew him and those who know of him.

Written by Lee Mumford in memory of his son.

for over six months awaiting a heart transplant before passing away on June 28, 2009, at the age of 41. In addition to several tennis scholarships established in his memory at his alma mater Vanderbilt University, the Keith Mumford Memorial Doubles Tournament hosted by Keith's home club CCV has become one of the most popular and meaningful events on the local tennis calendar.

As more fully described in a later chapter, the highlight of the Richmond tennis community in 2010 was surely the USTA's Best Tennis Town contest, which saw Richmond finish a strong third place behind Charleston, SC and Atlanta, GA, winning $25,000 for community tennis programs and facilities.

National accolades for local individuals and organizations continued in 2011. Lobs & Lessons was named a national NJTL chapter of the year. Former VCU standout and current Director of Tennis at Midlothian Tennis Club Feisal Hassan was named national Professional of the Year by the USPTA. Thanks to the encouragement of friends like Janine Underwood at USTA/Virginia and assistance from USTA/Mid-Atlantic leadership and staff, the RTA applied for, and won, a $100,000 USTA grant and recognition as a national target market for the promotion of 10 and Under Tennis.

2011 city champion Matt Waddell (l) with tournament director Tom Hood.

On the court, 2011 witnessed the first teenage victory in the men's city championship since David Caldwell in the 90s as Deep Run High School junior Matt Waddell took home the Einwick Cup by defeating Jeremy New in the finals of the Davenport city tournament.

Richmond has seen a few of its most talented juniors head south in recent years to train at Florida academies. Emily Hahn, the 2009 Richmond Times-Dispatch Female Player of the Year as a freshman at Douglas Freeman High School, spent the next two years at Nick Saviano's High Performance Academy in Florida honing her skills which earned her a high national ranking and a tennis scholarship at Princeton University. Chrissie Seredni, who won the Davenport city title as a 14-year old in 2002 and held a top five national ranking as a junior, moved to Bradenton, Florida, to better prepare her for the pro tour, where she played for several years before successfully regaining amateur status to play college tennis for Florida International. Callie Whitlock, who played No. 1 for St. Catherine's and teamed with Tatsiana Uvarova to win the Virginia State Indoor women's doubles crown in 2010, also spent time in Florida training at Rick Macci's Tennis Academy.

Kyle Parker, Max Schnur and Kevin McMillen kept alive Richmond's tradition of excellence on the national stage by bringing home first place trophies at national events—Kyle winning the 2008 Southern Open as an unseeded player before moving onto college to play for the College of Charleston under coach Jay Bruner, and Max Schnur winning two national open doubles titles and being named to the Mid-Atlantic Section Junior Davis Cup team before heading to college to play for the Columbia Lions in the Ivy League. Kevin McMillen, a four-time all-district player at Mills Godwin High School, captured a national doubles title at the Southern Open to highlight a superlative junior career. He currently plays on the men's tennis squad at George Mason University.

The 2011 Richmond Times-Dispatch All-Metro Tennis Team provides a great snapshot of some of the area's top junior talent in recent years. On the girls' side, there was Player of the Year Christine Abbott (Midlothian), Anna Fuhr (Steward School), Lauren Denuel (Cosby), Caroline Mosberg (Deep Run), Callie Whitlock (St. Catherine's) and Maddie Wood (Mills

Kyle Parker was another dominant player for the record-setting Mills Godwin High School tennis program.

Godwin). Fuhr pulled off the upset of the women's open division at the 2011 McDonald's Mid-Atlantic Clay Court Championships, defeating No. 3 seed Kateryna Yergina 6-3, 0-6, 6-3 in the first round on her way to a quarterfinal finish in the area's premier clay court event. Whitlock was named the Virginia Independent Schools Tennis Association Player of the Year in 2009 and led her St. Catherine's team to a state championship in 2010.

The boys' side included Player of the Year Max Schnur (Collegiate), Evan Charles (Deep Run), Hunter Koontz (Deep Run), Brett Moorhead (Cosby), Brady Straus (Collegiate) and Edgar Vitkovski (Mills Godwin). Koontz was a four-time All-Metro selection, 2010 Times-Dispatch All-Metro Player of the Year and capped his high school tennis career with an improbable three-peat — winning the Group AAA singles and doubles titles (with Evan Charles) and leading Deep Run to the state team championship.

The past few years have witnessed something of a rebirth of tennis activity and excitement at Battery Park and other public courts. Thanks to the efforts of the Metro Richmond Tennis Club, Richmond Racquet Club, the City's Department of Parks, Recreation, and Community Facilities, and volunteers like George Banks, Joe and Shima Grover, Guy Walton, and Fred Bruner, new clinics, tournaments, and other tennis activities are springing up at the public parks across town. The 10&Under tennis revolution taking place all over town is highlighted in another chapter.

In December 2011, the Westwood Club and Dr. Neal Carl hosted a special event sponsored by Glen Allen-based Star Scientific, Inc. and its CEO Jonnie Williams that featured an entertaining evening of tennis showcasing former top ten players Aaron Krickstein and Jimmy Arias (with a cameo appearance by Robert Seguso), along with comments from legendary tennis coach Nick Bollettieri.

There are so many takeaways from this brief chronology of Richmond tennis history. Perhaps most important is the powerful bond that a family can share through tennis. Tennis is truly the sport for a lifetime in that it can be enjoyed by family members of all ages. How many sports could offer Lindsay and Ginny Wortham the opportunity to play together (and win) national championships, as they did in 2010 at the USTA National Mother-Daughter Grass Court Championships in Newport, Rhode Island? It is telling that so many people who were active in the local tennis community as juniors, decide to return to Richmond after college to settle down, raise tennis families and remain active on the tennis scene. Passion and appreciation for the sport along with a strong commitment to community service are common threads that have fueled the growth and evolution of tennis in Richmond.

Ed and Leslie Butterworth, and Cris and Melissa Robinson, are great examples of two couples who found love through tennis and returned to Richmond after college to raise their families. Each one is a respected teaching pro, active volunteer and parent of emerging tennis stars. Richmond tennis has been blessed over the decades with many families like the Butterworths and Robinsons who can point to two, three—sometimes more—generations of tennis players and supporters who keep tennis thriving throughout the area. Tennis families like the Blairs, Bruners, Cains, Caldwells, Cummings, DePews, Einwicks, Fuhrs, Horsleys, Leitchs, Magners, Mumfords, Nimitzes, Parkers, Waters, Worthams and so many other great families have helped shape the course of Richmond tennis history over the years.

Star Scientific, Inc. and Neal Carl organized a special tennis exhibition in December 2011 at the Westwood Club featuring several tennis legends: (l to r) Robert Seguso, Nick Bollettieri, Neal Carl, Jimmy Arias and Aaron Krickstein.

CHAPTER 2

PEOPLE, TEAMS AND PROGRAMS

Several of Richmond's top women (from left) Margie Walsh, Kirsten Elim, Julie Ogborne, Leslie Butterworth and Rachel Gale represented the USTA/Mid-Atlantic Section in the 2011 National 35s Intersectional Championships in Boca Raton, Florida.

Arthur Ashe

By John Packett

Arthur Ashe holds one of the three WCT United Virginia Bank Tennis Classic championship trophies he won. *Courtesy of Richmond Times-Dispatch.*

When he was growing up and learning to play tennis in segregated Richmond in the 1950s and early 60s, Arthur Ashe was mostly an invisible man to the rest of the city.

Even though he was becoming quite proficient at hitting the fuzzy little ball around the court, Ashe's skin color kept him off the majority of the city's courts and therefore away from any strong competition with his white peers.

Ashe, of course, went on to become one of the top players in the world, won Wimbledon, the U.S. Open, the Australian Open and is the city's most well-known tennis figure, as well as one of Richmond's most beloved athletes.

But how could he have managed to learn the game so well and become so good at the sport without much robust opposition during his formative years? Especially in a time when very few African-Americans played tennis.

"He was such a good athlete," said Tom Chewning, a former chief financial officer of Dominion Resources, Inc., who became good friends with Ashe after they first met in 1959. "Maybe if he had been born in the inner city in New York, he would have played basketball."

Ashe was, in fact, also an excellent baseball player and a member of the team at Maggie Walker High School.

"He had the speed of a gazelle and a sharp batting eye," Dr. Francis M. Foster told the Richmond Times-Dispatch in an article after Ashe's death in 1993. Dr. Foster was one of the city's foremost authorities on the history of Richmond's black community.

According to Dr. Foster, Ashe was told during his sophomore year in high school to drop baseball so he could concentrate on tennis.

Having tennis courts right next to his home on the North Side was another distinct advantage for Ashe. His father, Arthur Ashe, Sr., got a job with the city as the supervisor of Brook Field playground when Ashe was four, and the courts were right outside his door.

Bill Redd grew up with Ashe and used to hit with him at Maggie Walker and the Brook Field courts.

"He was very good," recalled Redd, who was on the tennis team with Ashe at Maggie Walker for one year.

Redd recalled going to the Brook Field courts and watching Ashe hit with Ron Charity, who had a big influence on his game.

"[Charity] was the only person who could keep the ball going well enough [with Ashe]," said Redd. "He kept Arthur's game going."

Hitting with Ashe in high school wasn't exactly a pleasant experience for Redd.

"From a teen-age standpoint, it was horrible," said Redd. "I tried to keep up with him. He would tutor me. I liked tennis so much and I idolized him. But I couldn't imagine him being a star until he started playing white people."

Arthur with his dad, Arthur Sr. *Courtesy of Richmond Times-Dispatch.*

"Then he started beating them, too. After that, the sky was the limit."

Chewning was one of those white people who began to exchange strokes with Ashe on the Brook Field courts. But not until he found out who he was during a Middle Atlantic Junior Tournament in Wheeling, WV, in the summer of 1959.

"I went up to Oglebay Park in Wheeling with my best buddy, O.H. Parrish, to play in the Middle Atlantics," said Chewning. "Back then, they had 15s and 18s [age groups]. I was in the 15-and-unders and O.H. was in the upper group.

"I was looking for my name on the drawsheet, and right next to it was the 18s draw. I was looking for O.H. to be number one [seed], and there's Arthur Ashe Jr., Richmond, Virginia, as the No. 1. I'm like, 'That just can't be true.'"

"I said to him, 'I'm really embarrassed that I didn't know who you were.' And he said, 'Well, we're not covered in the paper. But I know who you are. I read all about you in the paper. I've seen your picture in the paper.'"

The two began practicing together at Brook Field on a regular basis, though Ashe was not able to join Chewning at Byrd Park, where most of Richmond's top young players learned under the tutelage of Sam Woods, because blacks were not allowed to play there until 1963.

"When I met him at 16, you would not have said at the time that he was on the elite level that he wound up," said Chewning.

Ashe got plenty of assistance during his early years from Dr. Robert "Whirlwind" Johnson, a Lynchburg physician who had helped two-time Wimbledon champion Althea Gibson, among other African-Americans, develop her game to a high level.

Johnson worked with Ashe on weekends and during the summers at his home in Lynchburg.

Ashe left Richmond to spend his senior year in high school in St. Louis, where he was able to compete against Wimbledon-champ-to-be Chuck McKinley, Clark Graebner and Butch Buchholz, three of the best young players in the country.

"When he came back at Christmas and we went over to hit, his game had gotten a good bit better," said Chewning, who noticed Ashe's play improved even more following his first semester at UCLA, which he attended on a tennis scholarship.

"He was like a different person. Then, his sophomore year, the UCLA team went to Australia, and he's playing [Ken] Rosewall and those guys."

Ultimately, what made Ashe better than most of his contemporaries was his amazing ability to focus on the court. And that was something he learned at an early age from his father – to remain calm and cool on the court no matter what the circumstances.

"He concentrated very well," said Chewning. "He didn't let things distract him. He just kind of built this wall, where that court was his sanctuary and he could control his own thoughts and his own actions."

"His dad had drilled into him that, 'Arthur, you aren't just a tennis player, you're a black tennis player and anything you do is going to reflect not only on our family but our race.' "

"He had a good athletic ability and his hand-eye coordination was fantastic. He had a pretty good amount of speed. He didn't beat himself like other players did. He was under control emotionally. And I think he got the most out of his game."

Ashe certainly proved all of that during his illustrious career, which ended prematurely after he suffered a heart attack in 1979.

Chewning feels there was also one more element that helped Ashe succeed on the court – his strong intellect.

"He was a really smart guy," said Chewning. "There's a lot of strategy in tennis and there's the

Ashe's game advanced quickly because he had courts near his home.

From left: Lou Einwick, Arthur Ashe and Jeanne Moutoussamy Ashe at the Richmond Coliseum.

hand-eye coordination. Moving the feet. There's also the person-to-person competition. It's a little bit of a chess match."

"I think tennis fit Arthur's intellectual interest and his personality really well. It was a game that sucked him in. Just had all the things to it that excited him."

Ashe used his influence off the court to champion many civil-rights causes over the years. The game he was attracted to at a young age gave him a platform that he never could have imagined from such humble beginnings.

Arthur Ashe At A Glance

Name: Arthur Robert Ashe, Jr.
Born: July 10, 1943 in Richmond, VA
Attended: Maggie Walker High School and UCLA, where he graduated in 1966.

Davis Cup: First black player to be named to the U.S. squad in 1963. He was a member of the team for 11 years and served as captain from 1981-85. His teams won back-to-back Davis Cups in 1981-82.

Grand Slams: Ashe won the first U.S. Open in 1968 as an amateur and was ranked No. 1 in the world. He captured the Australian Open in 1970 and upset Jimmy Connors to win the Wimbledon title in 1975.

NCAA: Singles and doubles champion in 1965; All-American from 1963-65.

Other accomplishments: Named Sports Illustrated Sportsman of the Year in 1992; author of several books, including "A Hard Road to Glory," a three-volume work which details the history of the black athlete in America; co-founder of the USTA's National Junior Tennis League.

Died: February 6, 1993, in New York City of complications from AIDS, a disease he contracted from a blood transfusion during heart surgery in 1983.

Yannick Noah (left) and Donald Dell help carry Ashe's casket from his service at the Arthur Ashe Center in Richmond. February 1993. *Courtesy of the Richmond Times-Dispatch.*

Arthur Ashe gave a number of clinics in his hometown, including this one at the Valentine Museum. *Courtesy of the Valentine Richmond History Center.*

Ashe Statue

By John Packett

When the idea of creating a statue to honor Arthur Ashe first took root in his mind in 1992, sculptor Paul DiPasquale wasn't sure how he wanted to fashion one of the city's most famous athletes.

So he decided to go right to the source – Ashe himself – to learn how the former Wimbledon and U.S. Open tennis champion wanted to be depicted in a lasting monument to his memory. And what message he would like to leave for the rest of the world to see and admire.

By the time DiPasquale was able to contact Ashe, however, he didn't have much longer to live as it turned out.

DiPasquale had met Ashe once briefly during a clinic with his daughter at Byrd Park in the spring of 1992.

"Based on that meeting, I wrote him a letter and told him, 'I'd like to do an authorized statue of you,'" said DiPasquale. "With your permission, of course. I'm going to call it the authorized and approved statue and seek to have it cast and bronzed and publicly displayed in Richmond."

Paul DiPasquale in front of his work in his studio.

At the time, there had been some discussion by city officials about the creation of an African-American Sports Hall of Fame in Richmond, based on Ashe's three-volume book "A Hard Road to Glory," which detailed the history of the black athlete in America.

The hall of fame never materialized but DiPasquale's intriguing and inspiring rendition of Ashe surrounded by children wound up on Monument Avenue, where it intersects with Roseneath Road, in the West End.

Ashe called DiPasquale in January, 1993, little more than two weeks before he died.

"One of the things he told me was he didn't want to be the center of the podium," recalled DiPasquale. "This is a monument, he said, that he wanted to be about children and about knowledge as the source of all our powers as human beings."

Before DiPasquale could meet with Ashe in New York about the project, he passed away on Feb. 6, 1993, at the age of 49.

"When I got back from the funeral [at the Arthur Ashe Center in Richmond], there was a package to me in the mail from A. Ashe in New York City," said DiPasquale. "I opened it and there were photographs we had spoken about from him.

"There was a little post-it note that simply said, 'Dear Paul. Wanted you to have these. Let's talk soon. A. Ashe.'"

From that point on, DiPasquale felt he was destined to work on the statue and have it installed either in Richmond or another city to honor the legacy of a man who was so much more than a tennis player on the world stage.

With the help of Ashe's wife, Jeanne, and other family members, DiPasquale was able to come up with a monument that was mutually agreeable to everyone, and the statue was unveiled on July 10, 1996, which would have been Ashe's 53rd birthday.

The bronze image reveals Ashe, in a warm-up suit with his shoes unlaced, holding a racket in one hand and books in the other, with four children staring up at him, eager to learn some of the life lessons that shaped his life.

There were strenuous objections to having the statue on Monument Avenue, which is the same thoroughfare that features four monuments to heroes of the Confederacy, of which Richmond served as the capital during the Civil War.

But City Council ultimately approved the location, and it continues to serve as a beacon to all those who gaze upon it.

"The first thing out of his mouth was children are our future," said DiPasquale of Ashe's idea about the monument. "Their education and their appreciation of books and knowledge as the building blocks of their future."

"He said, 'This [tennis] was my trade. This is what I built but I wouldn't have built it without education, dedication, and discipline to my field.'"

2011 Richmond Tennis Association
Board of Directors

RTA Presidents

1954-1955	Cy Slavin	1983-84	Bill Walker
1956	Henry Valentine	1985-86	Sue Cain
1957	Bobby Leitch	1987-88	Lindsay Wortham
1958-59	J.A. Gunter	1989	Lou Einwick
1960-61	Harold Jones	1990-91	Irving Driscoll
1962-63	Massie Valentine	1992-93	Debbie Pomeroy
1964	Frank Maloney	1994-95	Tom Vozenilek
1965-66	Lou Einwick	1996	Sharon Jensen
1967-68	John Kenny	1997-98	Michael Pratt
1969	Waller Horsley	1999-2000	Matt Schon
1970-71	Skip Forrest	2001-03	Fred Bruner
1972-73	Gayle Marlow	2004-06	Eric Perkins
1974	John Oakey	2007	Stuart Horsley
1975	Reb McCowen	2008	Fred Bruner
1976	Jerry DePew	2009-10	Hugh Waters, III
1977-78	Paddi Valentine	2011	Eric Perkins
1979-80	Gaile Zfass	2012	Joe Grover
1981-82	Anne Miller		

Richmond Tennis Association

By Eric Perkins

The junior tennis scene in Richmond in the 1940s and 1950s centered around Sam Woods and his tennis program at Byrd Park. The biggest challenge facing Woods and his students was financial support (the city allotted only a small sum of money, a counselor, and one assistant to support Sam Woods' tennis programs), and this funding gap was the catalyst that led to the formation of the Richmond Tennis Association.

The first incarnation of a local community tennis association was organized in 1946 to promote junior tennis, but that organization disbanded after less than a decade. The Richmond Tennis Patrons Association, later shortened to the Richmond Tennis Association ("RTA"), was incorporated in 1954 for the purpose of encouraging the development of junior tennis in the Richmond area. The RTA provided critical funding, leadership, and volunteer support for junior tennis throughout the community, and while the organization expanded its scope over the years to provide programming and events for players of all ages and levels, it has never strayed too far from its original focus on junior tennis and community service.

As a community service organization, the RTA has racked up many prestigious awards over the years at the state, sectional and national levels, including a national community service award from Pepsi Cola in 1965 and the USTA Organization of the Year award in 1993. Although the RTA has always been a volunteer-based organization, at various times in its illustrious history it has benefitted from the paid services of talented and dedicated individuals who served as Executive Director. Lou Einwick served the longest tenure as Executive Director from 1998 to 2007 after serving on the board of directors for over 30 years (including two terms as President). Kirsten Elim, Linda Larue, Kathy Lawrence, Sheri Crowell, Patty Smith and Bridget Reichert have also served the organization well in this critical role over the years. In 2010, the RTA also hired Lisa Deane as a part-time Director of Communications and Programming to help build awareness throughout the community, identify and pursue new funding opportunities, and develop new strategic partnerships.

The RTA has played an important role in promoting tennis and sportsmanship throughout the community. On July 22, 1963, the RTA voted to allow African Americans to compete in RTA-sponsored tournaments, marking a pivotal break from the "whites only" policy that had been followed by many area tennis facilities and tournament organizers in that era. This was more of a public policy statement since there had never been a written policy restricting tournament participation on the basis of race, but local traditions and social norms had largely prevailed up to that point.

From left: Former RTA President Gaile Zfass, Arthur Ashe and then-current RTA President Ann Miller chat during a break at the RTA's Annual Meeting in 1980. *Courtesy of Richmond Times-Dispatch.*

With the debut of the area's first indoor tennis facility at the Westwood Club in 1967, the RTA was able to establish a formal winter development program for top juniors. The program continued in some form for the better part of the next fifty years and was a significant factor in the development of a slew of nationally ranked juniors (several of whom went on to play on the professional tour and many more who went on to play at the collegiate level).

Funding during the early years of the organization came largely from membership dues, contributions and net proceeds from Jack Kramer's barnstorming troupe that would come to town periodically for an evening of professional tennis. Local tennis fans came out in droves to these events in the 1950s and 1960s to see tennis legends such as Bobby Riggs, Pancho Segura, Frank Sedgman, Frankie Parker and Pancho Gonzales, among many more. Other clinics and exhibition matches organized by the RTA during this period featured Fred Stolle, Ian Crookenden, Chuck McKinley, Cliff Drysdale, and Maureen Connolly. Local tennis legends Arthur Ashe and Bitsy Harrison would also return to Richmond and participate in many clinics and special events over the years.

Under the stewardship of Lou Einwick, the RTA was instrumental in helping establish Richmond's longest running professional tennis tournament, which had a successful 19-year run and became the RTA's primary fundraiser. The tournament is described in more detail in another chapter.

By 1975, Richmond was home to no less than nine juniors holding top ten national rankings, including Mark Vines, Tommy Cain, Neal Carl, Junie Chatman, Rodney Harmon, and Kathleen Cummings. Richmond's dominance was even more striking at the sectionals, as evidenced by the number of Richmond juniors holding top 10 sectional rankings in 1975:

Men's Open
Junie Chatman #8

Boys 18s
Tommy Cain #1
Bobby Fauntleroy #8
David Hawkins #9

Boys 16s
Marell Harmon #1
John DePew #4
Alan Butler #5

Boys 14s
Rodney Harmon #2
Michael Reynal #9

Boys 12s
Scott Hendrickson #5
Grif Blackard #6

Women's Open
Flo Bryan #7

Girls 16s
Lloyd Hatcher #3
Betty Baugh Harrison #4
Kathleen Cummings #5

Girls 14s
Kathleen Cummings #5
Margie Waters #10

Girls 12s
Stacy Moss #4
Carol Koehler #10

Cain recalls that one of his first tastes of big-time junior tennis came when he was 11 years old and the RTA sent him to train for a week at Harry Hopman's tennis academy in Port Washington, NY, where he was housed by the McEnroe family. Recognizing its status as a national hotbed for top junior tennis, the U.S. State Department selected Richmond to host a stop on a special tour for outstanding tennis players from around the world. Aside from financial and coaching support, the RTA sponsored local teams and competitions such as the

Junior Wightman Cup and helped bring national junior events to Richmond such as the USTA Intersectional Championships.

> "I never cease to be amazed by the tireless work of the community of volunteers that made and continue to make Richmond a great tennis town."
>
> — Tom Cain
> Richmond Tennis Hall of Fame Member

Throughout much of its history, the RTA was active in running junior tournaments at all levels—local, state, sectional, and national—to foster more and higher-level competitive play opportunities for local juniors. From 1977-1980, the RTA ran a national invitational junior event sponsored by Life of Virginia that brought many of the nation's top 18-under and 16-under players to town. For a six-year period in the 1980s, the RTA also helped promote a men's professional satellite tour event at Brandermill.

In the 1990s, the RTA continued to be an active and innovative force in the tennis community. Under the leadership of President Tom Vozenilek, the RTA created a new club-based team event known as the Club Challenge. This event, sponsored initially by Trigon (now Anthem), quickly grew to become a primary fundraiser for the RTA and one of the largest and most-anticipated tennis events in town. The organization was instrumental in creating the Capitol Area Tennis Hall of Fame (later renamed the Richmond Tennis Hall of Fame), electing classes of inductees in 1990, 1995, and 1997. The RTA also orchestrated an international student exchange program that saw several local families host Bosnian high school students who made an immediate splash on the local tournament and high school tennis scenes.

The 21st century has witnessed the continued evolution of the RTA. While it still organizes and operates the Davenport city tennis tournament—one of the longest-running city tournaments in the nation—by 2003, the RTA had largely abandoned the active management of junior tournaments, preferring instead to play more of a supporting role and shifting those opportunities to area tennis clubs. The RTA officially entered the world of social media networking in 2005 with the debut of www.richmondtennis.org. Facebook pages and Twitter accounts would soon follow.

New programs, events, strategic relationships have emerged to widen the presence and influence of the RTA in the community. Wheelchair tennis, QuickStart tennis, and adult and junior team tennis leagues, are just a few of the new activities being added to the RTA's resume. Under the leadership of RTA board member Tom Hood, the RTA resurrected the Richmond Tennis Hall of Fame, inducting new classes at sold-out dinner ceremonies in 2009 and 2011. It was only natural that the RTA spearheaded the city's bid in 2010 to participate in the USTA's Best Tennis Town contest.

Not limiting its financial support to junior programming and development, the RTA has also contributed funds over the years to refurbish public courts around town, particularly Byrd Park, and support local tournaments being run by other organizations. The RTA has also diversified its fund-raising efforts, pursuing grant opportunities with increasing success both locally and nationally. In November 2011, the USTA announced Richmond as a special target market for the growth and development of 10 and Under Tennis, a tremendous honor that included $100,000 in funding support over a 3-year period.

Throughout its history, the RTA has been blessed with strong support from the local business community. Fidelity Bankers Life, Central Fidelity Bank, United Virginia Bank, Thalhimers, Dominion National Bank, Home Beneficial Life Insurance Company, Massey, Wood, and West, C. P. Dean, NationsBank, Davenport and Company, Trigon Blue Cross/Blue Shield, Anthem and McDonalds have all been generous supporters of the RTA and community tennis over the years. More importantly, thousands of individuals have volunteered their valuable time and talent to the RTA over the years, and it is their shared passion for both tennis and community service that has made this organization successful and insured Richmond's spot as one of the top tennis towns in America.

> "This book illustrates the history of tennis in Richmond in such a detailed and interesting way. It is a great read for anyone who loves how a sport can positively impact an entire community."
>
> — Rodney Harmon
> Richmond Tennis Hall of Fame Member

2011 RTA junior award winners included (l to r) Liam Sullivan, Jacqueline Dillon, Harris Blair and Connor Brewer.

The RTA has always taken great pride in recognizing outstanding junior achievement and here are details concerning the RTA's slate of annual junior awards:

Ellen Smith Maloney Award
for Most Improved Girl

Ellen and her husband Frank were active RTA volunteers for many years, and Ellen was particularly active helping with RTA junior programs and events. This award was created in her memory in 1968 to recognize the area's most improved junior female.

1969	Lindsay Burn	1990	Shawn Arrowsmith
1970	Betty Baugh Harrison	1991	Christy Pomeroy
1971	Lloyd Hatcher	1992	Melissa Mason
1972	Martha Beddingfield	1993	Katherine Chen
1973	Heidi Markel	1994	Amy Fowler
1974	Anne Grubbs	1995	Bridget Bruner
1975	Kathleen Cummings	1996	Kristin Lanio
1976	Becky Oatts	1999	Kelly Kennedy
1977	Stacey Moss	2001	Lindsey Howard
1978	Leanne Seward	2002	Chrissie Seredni
1979	Martha Saine	2003	Britt Aspinall
1980	Tricia Holder	2004	Natalie Kretzer
1981	Diane Sancilio	2005	Katie Blow
1982	Bonnie Bunsavage	2006	Jessica Armes
1983	Valerie Farmer	2007	Callie Whitlock
1984	Stephanie Hiedemann	2008	Emily Hahn
1985	Leslie Seward	2009	Anna Fuhr
1986	Shannon Cubitt	2010	Christine Abbott
1987	Jane Wright	2011	Connor Brewer
1988	Kim Nance		
1989	Tinsley Mercer		

Greg Semon Award
Enthusiasm & Love for the Game

Greg Semon was a fun-loving junior active in RTA programs during his teenage years. Always an enthusiastic presence on and off the court with a smile you'd never forget, he passed away in his early twenties. His family worked with the RTA to create this annual award in 2001 honoring his memory.

2001	Ryan Mostrom
2002	John Snead
2003	Katherine Slagel
2004	Ken Nguyen
2005	Amanda Schubert
2006	Corey Pegram
2007	Kevin Calhoun
2008	Kevin McMillen
2009	Brady Straus
2010	Tyler Carey
2011	Justin Cerny

Dorothy Chewning Award
Enthusiasm & Love for the Game

Dorothy was an RTA board member and an officer for several years and active in organizing the Virginia Slims women's pro tour event at Westwood in the early to mid 1970s. This award is named in her memory to recognize the girl who demonstrates the most enthusiasm and love for tennis.

2008	Nicole Parker
2009	Michele Ackerman
2010	Anne Peyton Leitch
2011	Allie Straus

Richard B. Passloff
Sportsmanship Award

Richard was active in the RTA, particularly its junior programs and the WCT pro tournament. He served a term as Vice President and was President-elect when he passed away in 1972. This award was created shortly thereafter in his memory to recognize a local junior who demonstrates the highest standards of good sportsmanship. Beginning in 2008 this became the male sportsmanship award.

1972	Junie Chatman	1991	Charles Einwick
1973	Brad Baylor	1992	David Caldwell
1974	Brian Gager	1993	Ian Boettcher
1975	Marell Harmon	1994	Kelly Smith
1976	Fernando Lightfoot	1995	David Rauschburg
1977	Leanne Seward	1996	Jay Bruner
1978	Leonard Booker	1999	Mary Ellen Lahy
1979	Sandra Beddingfield	2001	Patrick Gee
1980	Rob Pinkham	2002	Cathy Nimitz & John Lanier
1981	Sonny Dearth	2003	Kate Harrington
1982	Rozzell Lightfoot	2004	Katie Harris
1983	Stephanie Baker	2005	Kristin Nimitz
1984	Larry Garrard	2006	Anne Garland
1985	Dondi Whitaker	2007	Arjun Karthikeyan
1986	Kim Boemer	2008	Colin Elliott
1987	Kevin Long	2009	Evan Charles
1988	Jane Wright	2010	Michael Holt
1989	Christy Pomeroy	2011	Harris Blair
1990	Cris Robinson		

Sue Cain
Sportsmanship Award

Sue was a former women's city champion, active for many years with the RTA (serving as President in 1985-86), and one of the leading female tennis officials in the world. Sue is a member of Mid-Atlantic Section Hall of Fame and the Richmond Tennis Hall of Fame, along with many other accolades in the tennis community. This award was created in her honor several years ago to recognize a local junior female who demonstrates the highest standards of good sportsmanship.

2008	Lilly Ellick
2009	Callie Whitlock
2010	Maddie Wood
2011	Jacqueline Dillon

Sam Woods Award
Most Improved Boy

This award was created in 1955 in honor of Sam Woods, known throughout the community as "Mr. Tennis" in the 1940s and 50s for his tireless efforts to promote tennis. He organized free junior programs at Byrd Park and was the coach of the Thomas Jefferson High School boys' tennis team, leading his teams to multiple state titles. This award originally recognized the area's most improved junior player, but later was changed to recognize the area's most improved junior male.

Year	Name	Year	Name
1955	Sarah Riley	1989	Sears Driscoll
1964	Mary Tompkins Miller	1990	David Caldwell
1966	Bill Correll	1991	Erik deVries
1968	Junie Chatman	1992	John Winter
1972	Butch Butcher	1993	Cary Broocks
1973	Hugh Waters, IV	1994	Todd Parker
1974	Bobby Fauntleroy	1995	Rhys James
1975	John DePew	1996	Joey Hopke
1976	Pat Perrin	1999	Austin Kim
1977	Rodney Harmon	2001	Robert Quinn
1978	Scott Hendrickson	2002	Brent Wilkins
1979	Steve Wilson	2003	Randy Loden
1980	Greg Miller	2004	Nick Moss
1981	Wade McGuire	2005	Jeremy New
1982	E. C. Eck	2006	Kyle Parker
1983	Kenny Thorne	2007	Zach Carl
1984	Carl Bell	2008	Brett Moorhead
1985	Ed Butterworth	2009	Hunter Koontz
1986	John Chichester	2010	Max Schnur
1987	Chris Davila	2011	Liam Sullivan
1988	Daniel Grinnan		

Hall of Famers

By Tom Hood

Despite all that Richmond had accomplished by 1990, RTA board member Tom Vozenilek identified a distinct void in the Richmond tennis community. Tom recognized Richmond would not be where it was if not for the dedication, both on and off the court, of some very special people. The Richmond Tennis Hall of Fame was born.

Initial eligibility requirements were pretty simple. A candidate had to have a minimum of 10 years since his or her first distinction involving tennis in the capital city area and fall into one of two categories, player or non-player. For the player category, consideration was based on a candidate's record of outstanding competitive achievement with consideration given to sportsmanship and character. For the non-player category consideration was given to those individuals or entities who or which made outstanding contributions based on service and dedication to the game.

Richmond Tennis Hall of Fame Class of 1990

Arthur R. Ashe, Sr.

In addition to his 25-year career with the City of Richmond, particularly in the Battery Park and Brook Field Park areas, Mr. Ashe devoted unlimited time and energy to the promotion of tennis at all levels. He was the head of operations for both the Fidelity/UVB Tennis Classic and the 1968 U. S. Davis Cup tie held at Byrd Park. Often he was seen offering assistance and encouragement to aspiring juniors. Mr. Ashe's contributions also include membership on the RTA Board of Directors as well as its Advisory Board, and in 1985 Mr. Ashe was honored by the RTA with a special award in appreciation of his service.

Arthur R. Ashe, Jr.

Arthur Ashe's accomplishments both on and off the court (chronicled earlier in this book) made him an obvious choice for the inaugural Hall of Fame class.

Dorothy W. Chewning

Ms. Chewning's efforts in developing women's tennis and her work in obtaining sponsorship from Philip Morris, Inc. were instrumental in the creation of the Virginia Slims professional women's tour. Ms. Chewning served as treasurer and a board member of the RTA, chairman of women's tennis rankings for the Virginia Tennis Association and a director of the women's division of the Westwood Racquet Club Indoor Invitational Tennis Tournament.

Louis C. Einwick, Jr.

Lou Einwick served more than forty years on the RTA board, including two terms as RTA president. He was also involved in the USTA/Mid-Atlantic Section and the Virginia Tennis Association. A certified referee and one of the founders of the Greater Richmond Tennis Umpires Association (GRTUA), Mr. Einwick was also chairman of the Fidelity/UVB Tennis Classic from 1966 to 1984. Mr. Einwick has been honored with numerous awards including the Service to Tennis Award by World Championship Tennis in 1985. He was inducted into the Mid-Atlantic Tennis Hall of Fame in 2002.

Samuel B. Woods

During World War II, Mr. Woods saw a pressing need to develop a program at Byrd Park for the youth of the city as well as programs for local adults and those stationed nearby due to wartime conditions. This initial part-time effort grew through the years to a full-time endeavor.

In 1944, Mr. Woods became the tennis coach at Thomas Jefferson High School and produced eleven state championship teams in his twenty years as coach. He took great pleasure in the large number of grassroots juniors who developed into recreational as well as competitive players, and he directed his energies to developing sportsmanship, physical fitness, and character in boys and girls alike.

Crestar Bank

When Crestar Bank, formerly United Virginia Bank, undertook co-sponsorship of the Fidelity/UVB Tennis Classic, the bank became a cornerstone in furthering the development and expansion of tennis programs in Richmond. From 1976 through 1984, the bank served as title sponsor of the event, underwriting over one million dollars in prize money. In addition, the bank donated tickets to numerous charities so that deserving youth, the disabled and minorities might have an opportunity to see "the greatest tennis in the world" played in Richmond. Crestar Bank continued to support and promote tennis in the Richmond area through its substantial contributions to the RTA's winter and year-round programs and tournaments.

Fidelity Bankers Life Insurance Company

In 1966, Fidelity Bankers Life Insurance Company joined with the RTA in its vision to take tennis to the Richmond public by bringing together world-ranked players in a tournament event, and the Fidelity Bankers Invitational Tennis Tournament was born. The event provided the impetus for future professional tournaments which would span the next eighteen years, as well as the economic means to provide much-needed equipment, training and travel money for the RTA's junior development program.

Class of 1995

Harold M. Burrows

Hal enjoyed a successful college tennis career and was the Virginia State men's champion from 1946 to 1948. In 1954, Burrows was selected to represent the United States as a member of the U.S. Davis Cup Team. Hal's tennis career reflects an impressive list of accomplishments. He is a member of the International Lawn Tennis Club, and he served on the Advisory Board of the Richmond Tennis Association. Burrows was the Director of Tennis at The Homestead for eleven years before becoming the Director of Tennis at The Country Club of Virginia for eighteen years. He was inducted into the Virginia Sports Hall of Fame in 1990 and the Mid-Atlantic Tennis Hall of Fame in 1992.

Susan S. Cain

An avid tennis player, Sue Cain was a Richmond City women's singles and doubles champion. Cain's interest in becoming a tennis official developed as her children entered local junior tournaments. She quickly moved up the "tennis officiating ladder" until Sue was recognized as a superior tennis official and was selected as a chair umpire at the U.S. Open for seventeen consecutive years. She also officiated at Wimbledon, the Australian Open and the 1988 Seoul Olympics. She also served as a chair umpire in the United Virginia Bank Tennis Classic in Richmond. Sue served terms as president of the Richmond Tennis Association, president of the Virginia Tennis Association and secretary of the USTA/Mid-Atlantic Section. She also served as a presidential appointment to the United States Tennis Association's Executive Committee. She was inducted into the Mid-Atlantic Hall of Fame in 2002.

Waller H. Horsley

Waller Horsley was a tennis champion at the junior, high school and collegiate levels. He was also a three-time state doubles champion. Mr. Horsley was a member of the core group that organized and conducted the Fidelity/UVB Tennis Classic. He was also a founding member of the Greater Richmond Tennis Umpires Association (GRTUA) and one of the first recipients of the GRTUA Award. During the 1960s, Mr. Horsley served as a member of the Richmond Tennis Association Board of Directors and as RTA president in 1969. His sons, Stuart and Garrett, were both active participants in junior tournaments during the 1970s, and enjoyed national rankings while supporting their father in local father/son tournaments.

Robert E. Leitch

Robert "Bobby" Leitch was a five-time winner of the men's singles at the city tournament, holding the title from 1939 to 1941 and again in 1946 and 1947. In addition, he won five father/son city doubles titles with his sons Rob and John and was a two-time Virginia State doubles champion. To round out the family affair, Mr. Leitch and his wife, Adele, won the city mixed doubles title in 1968. Bobby was active as a tennis official, serving as chair umpire for Fidelity Bankers Life/UVB Tennis Classic. He was president of the RTA in 1957 and was active on the RTA Board of Directors for a number of years.

Dr. John Watson

Dr. John Watson was an active tennis player and held top rankings within the senior divisions of the American Tennis Association (ATA) and was a finalist in the senior division of the ATA Championships. Dr. Watson's greatest personal satisfaction came from the impact he had on children through tennis. He served as tournament director of the Southeastern Open tennis tournament for over forty years and secured numerous scholarships for his participants. Dr. Watson was instrumental in developing hundreds of juniors. Off the court, Dr. Watson served as president of the Richmond Racquet Club and first vice president of the ATA. He also served several terms on the RTA Board of Directors. He was the varsity tennis coach at Virginia Union University for thirty-seven years and a volunteer tennis director for the Richmond Department of Parks and Recreation. Dr. Watson was inducted into the Mid-Atlantic Tennis Hall of Fame in 1992.

Thalhimers

Thalhimers Department Store served as an outstanding corporate citizen of Richmond for over 150 years, dating back to 1842. At the request of Sam Woods, Thalhimers sponsored a men's tournament starting in 1950 that attracted many outstanding players. Winners included local stars Gene Wash, Chuck Straley, Del Sylvia, Bobby Payne, Bob Bortner and Bitsy Harrison. After the city tournament moved to Byrd Park in 1967, the tournaments were consolidated under Thalhimers sponsorship until the early 1990s.

Class of 1997

F. G. "Jerry" DePew

F. G. "Jerry" DePew was a mainstay in the Richmond tennis community. Jerry was the consummate volunteer, dedicating countless hours to the promotion of tennis for the Richmond area. For many years Jerry was a RTA board member, and he eventually served as its president. Jerry is also a past president of the Virginia Tennis Association and past president of the USTA/Mid-Atlantic Section. He was a member of the Virginia ranking committee and was the director of the Mid-Atlantic boys 18s and 21s tennis tournaments for many years. He represented Virginia as a delegate to the USTA/Mid-Atlantic Section and was instrumental in bringing the Life of Virginia Junior Invitational to Richmond in the late 1970s.

Frank C. Maloney, III

Frank C. Maloney, III played on the nationally ranked men's tennis team at Yale University. He continued to play tennis here in the Richmond area well into his 40s. He spent many years as an active board member of the RTA and served as its president. Frank was also a past president of the Virginia Tennis Association and an active tennis official. Frank was pleased to serve as one of the initial members of the executive committee for the Fidelity Bankers Life/UVB Tennis Classic. Frank sponsored the Ellen Smith Maloney Award for the RTA which is presented to a promising junior girl in the community.

E. Massie Valentine

Massie Valentine started playing tennis at an early age. He won the Boys 15 and under Virginia State singles and doubles championships in 1948 and was captain of his high school tennis team. Massie was also a member of the UVA tennis team from 1953 to 1955. His accomplishments on the tennis court were exemplary as he is the holder of five city doubles championships. Massie's success did not stop at the city level as he went on to win state doubles titles in 1963 and 1964. Later on he was active in helping to bring the Fidelity Bankers Life/UVB Tennis Classic to Richmond, and he was one of the initial members of its executive committee. Massie was an active member of the RTA, serving a term as its president.

Home Beneficial Life Insurance Company

Through the efforts of Mr. Richard Wilshire and Home Beneficial Life Insurance Company, the Home Beneficial Life Insurance Junior Tennis Tournament, fondly known as the "Home Benny," became known as one of the premier junior tournaments in the Mid-Atlantic Section. Many players used this tournament to prepare for upcoming sectional and national tournaments.

Class of 2009

Tom Cain

Tom Cain started playing tennis at the age of eight. As a teenager, he won consecutive city men's singles titles in 1976 and 1977 and ranked among the nation's top juniors in his age division. In 1976, he was a member of the U.S. Junior Davis Cup Team. Tom played collegiate tennis at Southern Methodist University where he earned All-American honors in 1980. He turned pro that year and had wins over Johan Kriek, John Sadri, Tim Mayotte, Sandy Mayer and Guy Forget during his playing career. Tom played professional tennis for six years and cracked the top 100 before injuries forced his retirement. Tom's experience on the pro tennis circuit has been invaluable as he has helped with the RTA junior development program and been active with other community tennis projects.

Kathleen Cummings

Kathleen burst upon the Richmond tennis scene in 1976 when, at the age of 14, she captured the women's singles title at the city tournament beating Lindsay Wortham in the final. Coached by her dad, former Salisbury Country Club tennis pro Jack Cummings, Kathleen went on to repeat as city champ in 1977 and win the Mid-Atlantic women's title the same year. In 1979, she claimed the women's singles title at the Virginia State Tennis Championship. Kathleen was a four-time collegiate All-American at Colorado and Texas. She reached the NCAA semifinals once before turning pro in 1984. During her professional career, her ranking was as high as #48 and she played all the major tournaments.

Rodney Harmon

Rodney Harmon's list of tennis accomplishments should be an inspiration to anyone involved with the sport. He began his junior tennis career through the local NJTL program. Assisted by RTA coaching and financial support, Rodney excelled on the junior tournament circuit - locally and nationally. He was Thomas Jefferson High School's #1 player, and he spent time honing his skills at the Bollettieri Tennis Academy in Bradenton, Florida. In 1980, he combined with University of Tennessee teammate Mel Purcell to win the men's NCAA doubles title. Rodney also played #1 singles at Southern Methodist University and was a two-time All-American. Rodney played professional tennis for several years during the 1980s, achieving a top 60 world ranking and reaching the quarterfinals of the 1982 U. S. Open. After a successful stint with the USTA where he held several senior positions, he now resides in Florida but returns to Richmond from time to time. His impact on the Richmond tennis scene will not be forgotten.

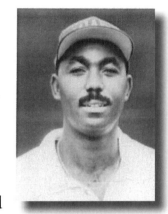

Wade McGuire

At an early age, Wade distinguished himself with his uncanny court sense, always seeming to know where to position himself for the next shot. A former city champion, Wade played #1 singles at the University of Georgia from 1991 to 1993 where he earned All-American honors each of those years. In 1992 and 1993, Wade was runner-up in the NCAA men's singles championships. Wade played on the pro tour for eight years and earned a career-high ranking of #163 in singles. He was a practice partner for the U.S. Davis Cup team in 1993 and 1994. After retiring from his playing career, Wade worked for the USTA on the women's coaching staff of the USA Tennis High Performance Program.

John Packett

John Packett covered tennis news for the Richmond Times-Dispatch from 1972 until his retirement in 2009. His first assignment was the city tournament. John was ever-present at the Virginia State Tennis Championships at Raintree Swim and Racquet Club, the Virginia State Indoors at the Country Club of Virginia and the McDonald's Mid-Atlantic Clay Courts at Salisbury Country Club. For twenty-five years he covered the U.S. Open in New York. He also covered the men's and women's pro tournaments during their heyday at the Richmond Coliseum and the Robins Center. Today, John is a freelance sports journalist and can still be found writing about local tennis news.

Mark Vines

Mark Vines won the men's city tournament three times, the Virginia State Tennis tournament's men's singles title four times and the Texas State men's singles title once. He played collegiate tennis at Southern Methodist University before joining the professional tour. During his playing career, Mark won the Paris Open Grand Prix Tournament in 1981. As a professional, Mark's ranking was as high as #110 in the world. After retiring from the pro circuit, Mark continued playing at the national level in age-group tournaments and has the distinction of being ranked #1 for his age in the 35s, 40s and 45s. In 2009, he won the National Clay and Grass Court Tournaments in the 50s age group. In 2012, he won the ITF Senior World Championship in the 55s age division.

Hugh C. Waters, III

Hugh Waters moved to Richmond in 1970 as the Director of Tennis at Westwood Racquet Club and the Richmond tennis community has never been the same. He later opened the very successful Richmond Tennis Academy and eventually bought Raintree Swim and Racquet Club. His enthusiasm for the sport is infectious and he has mentored an untold number of players, many of whom achieved rankings and competed on the national level. Some of his many accomplishments are: University of Florida Blue Key Leadership Society, USTA 1999 Family of the Year, Mid-Atlantic Tennis Hall of Fame (1995), Mid-Atlantic Tennis Association vice president, Mid-Atlantic USPTA president, Mid-Atlantic service award, Florida Section Family of the Year (1999), USTA/Mid-Atlantic Section Family of the Year (1984), Florida Section and USPTA Achievement award (2001).

Davenport & Company

A Richmond institution since 1863, Davenport & Company has long been associated with the local tennis community. Since 1998, the company has sponsored the Richmond City Tennis Championships. Through Davenport's commitment, the city tournament has been able to evolve and maintain its status as one of the area's premier tennis tournaments.

The Westwood Club

For many years The Westwood Club has been a staunch supporter of tennis in the Richmond area, hosting numerous events such as junior tournaments, collegiate tournaments, league championships, charity exhibitions and professional events. Home of the Anthem Challenge, the club has a strong tradition of promoting the growth and development of junior tennis.

Class of 2011

Fred Bruner

Playing number one for his high school team, Fred competed for district and regional titles and, upon graduation, earned the number one spot on the Hampden-Sydney College men's tennis team. He continued to play competitively after college but time was limited as he pursued his law degree. Fred's early experiences in tennis gave him the deep appreciation for what the sport has to offer and how much others may benefit from it. Fred became active with the RTA on an administrative level where he served as vice president for two years, and became the first person to serve as president for four years. Fred Bruner's many years of working with the city youth programs, running the Davenport Richmond City Tennis Championships, and continuing RTA involvement have made him Richmond's true tennis ambassador.

Junius "Junie" D. Chatman, Jr.

When he decided to turn his attention to tennis, it was not long before Junie was at the top in every one of his age divisions. His excellent high school record earned him a spot in Sports Illustrated's "Faces in the Crowd" section, and he received a full scholarship to perennial tennis power, the University of North Carolina. While at UNC, he was a four-time ACC champion and, upon graduation, Junie won the city men's singles title in 1978. He continued his career playing on European club pro teams and the professional tennis circuit, earning world rankings in both singles and doubles. In 1983, he won the Virginia State Tennis Championships and, in 1985, he won his second city title.

John W. "Bitsy" Harrison

Bitsy Harrison may arguably be one of the best players to have ever emerged from the Richmond area. Bitsy's incredible career dates back to the 1950s and 60s. Witness the following: Bitsy won the Richmond City championships, the Virginia State championships and the Middle Atlantic championships in the boys' 15 and under, boys' 18 and under, and men's open divisions. He played collegiately on the powerful University of North Carolina tennis team. Bitsy went on to play national tournaments where he reached a ranking in the USTA top twenty. Bitsy played in the U.S. Open at Forest Hills an amazing five years. Bitsy also played in the inaugural Fidelity Bankers Life Tennis Invitational, featuring eight of the country's top players, losing in a tight match to the eventual winner, Wimbledon champion Chuck McKinley.

Gayle H. Marlowe

Gayle Marlowe was an avid tennis player in the Richmond area. Her main contribution, however, was her dedicated service to the game. Active in all parts of Richmond tennis, she was a member of the RTA Board of Directors.

In 1972, Gayle was the first female president of the RTA. She also was a member of the executive committee for the professional tournament, the United Virginia Bank Tennis Classic. Gayle helped found and run the Life of Virginia National Junior Invitational Tournament. She was also in charge of the National Seniors Tournament at the Westwood Club which featured such players as Bobby Riggs.

Lindsay Burn Wortham

When one thinks of women's tennis in the Richmond area, the first name that comes to most people's minds is Lindsay Wortham. Lindsay competed in the city tournament for over twenty years, winning the championship three times: 1970, 1971 and 1981. She reached the final three other times, the last in 1991, an incredible twenty-one years after her first victory! Throughout the years Lindsay was extremely active in the Richmond Tennis Association. She ran the junior development program and held numerous offices including the presidency (1987 – 1988). In a testament to Lindsay's incredible athletic ability, she came out of tennis retirement in 2010 to play in a national mother-daughter championship with her daughter, Ginny, also a city champion. The two not only won their age group division but amazingly won the open division as well!

Anthem BlueCross BlueShield

The annual team competition held between Richmond area tennis clubs has become known as the "Anthem." Officially known as the "Anthem Challenge," the event has grown to over seven hundred participants and is the single largest tennis gathering in the Richmond area. Anthem BlueCross BlueShield has sponsored the event for nineteen years. Additionally, Anthem has been active with tennis events other than the Anthem Challenge, sponsoring a variety of events including senior tournaments and exhibitions featuring some of the world's greatest players. The successful events sponsored by Anthem BlueCross BlueShield were key factors in Richmond becoming one of America's best tennis towns!

Hall of Fame Class of 2009. (l to r) Wade McGuire, John DePew accepting for Jerry DePew, Rodney Harmon, Hugh Waters III, John Packett, Tom Cain, Kathleen Cummings, Massie Valentine, Mark Vines, Coleman Wortham accepting for Davenport & Company and Bill French accepting for the Westwood Club.

RTA President Eric Perkins (far right) and several members of the Hall of Fame Class of 2011 (l to r) Junie Chatman, Lindsay Wortham, Fred Bruner and Brian Marlowe accepting for Gayle Marlowe.

Richmond Tennis Notables

For some reason Richmond seems to be particularly blessed with individuals for whom tennis has become a part of their soul. Whether these people are playing it, writing about it, teaching it or organizing it they truly love the game and enjoy being around it. The following is a list of some (but certainly not all) of Richmond's tennis notables and their area of accomplishment.

George Banks
Coach, Volunteer

Eva Bard
Coach

Bill Barnes
Tournament Promoter, Sponsor

Bobby Bayliss
Coach

June Beddingfield
Volunteer

Irv Cantor
Volunteer

Tom Chewning
Player, Volunteer

Bill Correll
Player, Volunteer

Franklin Crawford
Junior Development

Sonny Dearth
Player, Media

Bill Deekens
Media

Michael and Elizabeth Fraizer
Volunteers, Sponsors

Lila Gilliam
Junior Leagues

Joe and Shima Grover
Volunteers

Ward Hamilton
Player, Volunteer, Facility Owner

Tom Hood
Player, Coach, Volunteer

Paul Kostin
Coach

Jerry Lindquist
Media

Anne Miller
Volunteer

Wayne Motley
Player, Volunteer

Eric Perkins
Volunteer

John Royster
Official

Georgia Saunders
Official

Paddi Valentine Waters
Volunteer

Tom Vozenilek
Volunteer

Bill Walker
Coach, Volunteer

Guy Walton
Coach

Mark Wesselink
Coach

Jim Wood
Volunteer

Gail Zfass
Volunteer

Great High School Teams

By John Packett

The Richmond area has long been a mecca for high school tennis in Virginia.

Thomas Jefferson High School began the tradition in the 1940s, and it has continued through Midlothian, Douglas Freeman, Clover Hill, Deep Run and, most recently, Mills Godwin, which holds the record for most titles in the girls division.

TJ is the all-time boys' leader with 15 state titles, one more than Maury. TJ and Maury won most of their titles before the AAA classification was instituted in 1971. Godwin is tied for third with 13 state crowns (eight in AAA and five in AA).

The Godwin ladies have won nine state championships, all but one under the direction of coach Mark Seidenberg.

Fourteen of TJ's titles came in what was known in those days as Division I or I-A. The last one was in Group AAA in 1971.

The latest Richmond-area school to bring home a state trophy is Deep Run, which has captured the past two boys' crowns (2010-11) behind strong teams led by Hunter Koontz, Evan Charles and Matt Waddell.

"Obviously, it's got to be the feeder system," said Seidenberg. "The local clubs. I think Raintree [Swim and Racquet Club] is the main club and there are others, too. Raintree has had indoor courts forever and kids are able to train there during the winter."

"There are just so many good junior programs out there … and we've been fortunate to reap the benefits."

At the beginning, though, was Sam Woods, who taught several generations of Richmonders the game at Byrd Park and was the tennis coach at Thomas Jefferson from 1944 through his death in 1963. Woods' teams won 11 straight championships from 1948-58.

The 1951 state champion Thomas Jefferson High School boys team. From left: Coach Sam Woods, Hart Grundy, Lanny Ross, Bob Bortner, Gene Wash, Gene Gee, Bobby Payne, Benet Gellman and Eddie Phillips.

"To begin with, he was an excellent player in his own right," said Jim Denoon, who played under Woods at TJ. "He just had a tremendous amount of tennis experience, and gave you a love of the game. He always had a pat on the back for you."

"He was a good coach and a good judge of talent. Through his program at Byrd Park, he was just waiting for you to come up and get in high school so you could be on the high school team. He developed his own feeder system."

The list of players for TJ under Woods reads like a who's who of local tennis. Among the stars were O.H. Parrish, Del and Bruce Sylvia, Bobby Payne, Bobby Bortner, Gene Wash, Wayne Adams, Eddie Phillips, Bitsy Harrison, Tom Chewning and Sam Woods Jr.

Becky Oatts starred for Douglas Freeman High School in the mid 70s. *Courtesy of Richmond Times-Dispatch.*

Craig Cooley (center) coached the Thomas Jefferson High School boys team in the 70s. Pictured with Coach Cooley are Nat Lee (left) and David Riggin (right).

The 2009 Collegiate girls state championship team.

The 1971 title marked the end of the TJ reign, as busing and integration caused most of the top players to transfer to county schools. Richard McKee headed a strong lineup in those days, along with Charlie Shiflett and the Leitch brothers, John and Rob.

The next area dynasty was Midlothian coached by Rick Crane, which won five straight titles from 1977-81. Among the top players during those years were John DePew, Steve Wilson, Barney Wilson, Greg Miller, Rob Pinkham, Hal Greer and Jeff Jones.

Douglas Freeman took over in the 1980s, claiming three championships between 1982 and 1989 behind Damian Sancilio, Ed Butterworth, Scott Pennington, Daniel Grinnan, Clint Greene and David Gibbs.

The high-flying Eagles of Mills Godwin, which had captured five straight Group AA crowns in the 1980s behind Kenny Thorne and Wade McGuire, moved up to Group AAA and eventually began dominating the largest classification, too.

Under the direction of coach Tom Hoy, who guided the Eagles from their inception in 1980 until he announced after the 2011 season that he was stepping down, Godwin claimed eight Group AAA championships.

The 2002 Mills Godwin state champion boys team lead by Coach Tom Hoy (top left).

"The proximity to Raintree allowed kids to have a year-round facility," said Hoy. "They've always been a junior-friendly club. So [players] came to Godwin having a good background. It wasn't like we had to do a whole lot with them."

"Because we had all that success early, it became the thing to do. You play tennis at Godwin, you get a little recognition. Even though they were good athletes and could have played other sports, tennis was an OK thing to do."

"The other key is we've always had really, really deep teams. We were usually very, very good at the bottom of the lineup."

Hoy ended his career with 471 victories, the most by any high school coach in Virginia.

Among the leading players for Godwin during its Group AAA run include Aljosa Piric, Igor Jekauc, Edin Terzimehec, Todd and Brock Parker, Charles Einwick, Matt Magner, Cris Robinson, Brent Wilkins, Ian Boettcher, Randy and Kevin Loden, Kevin Calhoun, Chad Harrell, Kyle Parker and Kevin McMillen.

On the girls side, Midlothian, Douglas Freeman and Clover Hill have won titles but Godwin has been the dominant force under Seidenberg. A few of Seidenberg's top players have included Kate Harrington, Lindsey Howard, Katie Blow, Nicole Parker, Maddie Wood, Kelly Stewart and Haley Moses.

The Eagles captured seven of nine state titles during one stretch, before their run ended in the 2011 final to First Colonial.

St. Christopher's and Collegiate, two of Richmond's premier private schools, added to the lists of champions with some top teams of their own. Tommy Cain, Ron Cain, Bobby Fauntleroy, Chris Blair, Ranny Fauntleroy, Stuart Horsley, Garrett Horsley, Jimmy Cain, Forest Butler, Alan Butler and David Hawkins led St. Chris, while Neal Carl, Tony Velo and Bill Correll headed Collegiate. The St.Christopher's team was especially dominant in the 70s and 80s, led at various times by the Eck brothers, Mumford brothers, Alec Forrest, Scott Davila, Eddie Phillips, Mark Troxell, Cole Durrill, John Chichester, Ward Marstiller, Matt Farley, David Caldwell and Paul Caldwell. From 1976 through 1991, St. Chris won 16 straight Prep League titles, as well as the National Interscholastic Championship in 1977.

Dedicated at a special ceremony in the fall of 2011, the Collegiate School's Williams-Bollettieri Tennis Center arguably represents the area's finest high school tennis facility and will provide a suitable home to one of Richmond's top high school tennis programs for years to come (e.g., the boys team, led by 2011 Prep League Coach of the Year Chris Conquest and VISAA Player of the Year Max Schnur, went 17-1 in 2011 with a Prep League championship and VISAA runner-up finish to its credit. The girls team, led by coaches Karin Whitt and Sharon Johnson and top players Connor Brewer and Ellie Whitlock, finished its most recent regular season with a 16-2 record and has won no less than 14 League of Independent Schools championships over the past 17 years).

Mark Seidenberg (right) and Asst. Coach Mary Bruner (left) with the Mills Godwin 2009 state championship team.

Great College Teams

By John Packett

The Richmond area, which has produced strong collegiate tennis teams through the years, outdid itself on two occasions.

In 1982, the University of Richmond captured the Association for Intercollegiate Athletics for Women (AIAW) national championship at the Division II level. The Lady Spiders finished first in a 24-team tournament, which was held in Greeley, Colorado.

Virginia Commonwealth University's men's team almost duplicated the feat at the Division I level, reaching the NCAA final in 2000 behind All-Americans Daniel Andersson and Frank Moser before losing to top-ranked Stanford 4-0 in Athens, Georgia.

Expectations were high for the Spiders in 1982, since they had been the AIAW runners-up in 1981 with a record of 27-5 – and they returned all but one player. UR also had many of the same players in 1980, when the Spiders wound up 10th nationally.

Two of those returnees were from Richmond, Martha Beddingfield and Sharon Dunsing.

"It was kind of the perfect storm," said Dunsing, who played No. 3 singles. "We had all the right pieces in place. The timing was right. We worked our way up those three years. We could sort of see what was happening and that we could do something big."

Martha Beddingfield (left) and Sharon Dunsing reunited years after leading University of Richmond to a national title.

"That [winning championship] became our goal, and it ended up working out, which was awesome. Everything fell into place."

1982 AIAW Division II national champions.

Under coach Eric O'Neill, UR went 23-5 and beat every Division I team in the state, including Virginia and Virginia Tech, en route to the national tournament. Among the schools in the national field were Boston College, Notre Dame, William and Mary and Georgetown.

"You never know how you're going to do," said Beddingfield, who played No. 1 singles and teamed with Dunsing as the No. 1 doubles team. "Tennis is a funny sport. But it [winning national title] was definitely one of our goals as a team."

"The reason our team was so good is that we had great athletes. They continued to improve in college because they were such good athletes. Not only did they understand how to play singles, but we had some good doubles players."

Both Beddingfield (three times) and Dunsing (two) went on to capture their share of Richmond city singles championships.

"I just remember it was nerve-wracking," said Dunsing. "It was three or four days of keeping track of points and scores, and knowing we were actually in the running to win it. Nothing was guaranteed but we felt good about it. It was pretty crazy when we won it."

UR moved up to the Division I level the following year, and the NCAA began to run women's sports shortly thereafter. While the Spiders haven't come close to the finals again, under the long-time leadership of Coach Mark Wesselink they have won eight Atlantic 10 titles in the past 10 years to qualify for the NCAAs.

The fact that VCU was included in the men's draw for the 2000 tournament was no surprise. After all, the Rams made the field 18 times during coach Paul Kostin's first 21 years at the school and were ranked 19th going into the 2000 event.

"We were kind of knocking on the door for a couple of years there before," said Kostin. "Suddenly we won a couple of close matches."

The first close one came in the second round, when the Rams knocked off No. 13 Mississippi 4-3 in Blacksburg, advancing to the Sweet 16 in Athens. VCU had had no trouble with Virginia 4-0 in the opening round.

VCU's next nail-biter came in the round of 16, where the Rams were down 3-2 before edging San Diego State 4-3.

That set up a quarterfinal against fourth-ranked Illinois, and the Rams found themselves trailing 3-1 before rallying to pull out another 4-3 victory. Frank Moser, at No. 2 singles, claimed the deciding point against the Illini, winning 7-6 in the third set.

In the semifinals, VCU ran into perhaps their toughest opponent yet in Tennessee and again fell behind 3-2. This is where it really got interesting, because the Rams won 4-3 when two Volunteers went down with cramps and had to default their matches.

"That match is kind of famous," said Kostin, "because we never really finished the match because two of their players cramped up, so we won. They couldn't finish their matches. When you go to Sweet 16, you play every day for four days."

Frank Moser is carried off the court after VCU completed a 4-3 upset of the University of Illinois at the 2000 NCAA tournament.

"It was one of those times when it was really hot down there. It was over 100 degrees. My guy was cramping, too, against Tennessee. He ended up in the hospital the day before the final. Now, they have one day in between the matches. You get a break."

The victory over Tennessee put VCU in the final against Stanford, where the Rams were no match for the Cardinals.

"We had grueling matches every day in 100 degrees, 4-3, 4-3, 4-3, and Stanford was cruising, 4-0, 4-0, 4-0. It makes a difference. But I tell you, we had a lot of luck, because we could have easily been out in the second round. Sometimes, things are going your way."

The Rams wound up with a final ranking of ninth in the country, the best in school history.

"I really think it meant a lot to college tennis in Virginia," said Kostin. "Before that, we were beating all the Virginia schools, but after that, and everybody was saying VCU goes to the NCAA final, there's no reason why U.Va. and Virginia Tech couldn't do similar things."

"So they hire good coaches and they got competitive and they got better. It comes down to putting more emphasis on the sport."

Feisal Hassan (left) and Jamie Hevron (center) were key contributors for the VCU men's team in the mid 1980s.

Public Parks

By Tom Hood

Truth be known, the beauty of tennis is that it is an every man's sport. All one needs is a tennis racket, tennis shoes and some balls and he or she is ready to go. With hundreds of public courts spread throughout the Richmond area, ANYONE can find a place to play. Over the years, however, there have been four main venues where people play at public parks, and play they do: Battery Park, Westover Hills, and Byrd Park in the city of Richmond, and Belmont Park in Henrico County.

Battery Park. Mention the name to a Richmond area tennis player and you are liable to be greeted with a long slow grin because you helped jar the fond memory of a not too distant past of playing in the Southeastern Open Tennis Tournament.

A mention of Battery Park might also have someone remembering the days when the American Tennis Association held its national championship there with the top African American players competing including Althea Gibson and Juan Farrow.

Mention Battery Park and the word resilience also comes to mind. Not even Mother Nature will keep it down long. In 2004, Battery Park was hit by flooding. It was buried with water, mud and sewage, and many thought Battery Park was gone for good. Not so. Within two years the sludge was cleared, the courts re-surfaced, new drainage installed, and Battery Park was back in business.

Did you know how much tennis talent came from Battery Park's courts? Not only did Arthur Ashe once play there but Richmond Tennis Hall of Famers Junie Chatman, Jr., and Rodney Harmon honed their skills on Battery Park's storied courts. Collegians Marell Harmon, Leonard Booker, Wayne Motley and Rozzell Lightfoot called Battery Park home as well.

Battery Park continues to thrive today mainly due to Dr. Watson's tremendous legacy. Guy Walton, a colleague and student of Dr. Watson's, not only runs the Southeastern Open, he also coaches Virginia Union University's tennis team. Guy also runs summer programs for the city of Richmond at Battery Park as well as the Richmond Racquet Club, a tennis program for rising junior players. George Banks, another of Dr. Watson's protégés, is coach of the Armstrong High School tennis team. George makes Battery Park home for his group, the Metro Richmond Tennis Association, another successful junior development program. In 2011, Battery Park hosted a USTA grass roots tournament series that was selected Tournament of the Year by the USTA/Mid-Atlantic Section. Ah, yes, Battery Park. The memories continue.

Before the USTA leagues were formed, THE team competition in Richmond was the Saturday morning Racket League Championship. Winning it brought not only recognition but great respect throughout the tennis community. In the early 1970s, Westover Hills offered the perfect venue for a group of recently graduated tennis enthusiasts. Tucked behind the shops at Westover Hills Boulevard and Forest Hill Avenue, Westover Hills had eight beautiful lighted tennis courts offering play well into the evening and which were used for various tournaments including the city tournament as well as high school matches. Jim Robertson, David Carter,

Jim Bodenheimer, Larry Loving, Jim Liles, David Baur, Bob Vick and Charlie Weston were the mainstays of these tennis enthusiasts and formed the nucleus of the Saturday morning Racket League team that put Westover Hills on the tennis map. The Westover Hills team won the Racket League championship three times in the early 70s defeating other more notable clubs. In recent years the courts have not seen the amount of activity they did in years past. There is discussion, however, that one or some of the courts may be used for USTA's acclaimed 10 and Under QuickStart Tennis programs.

Belmont Park, formerly the site of Hermitage Country Club, is a Henrico County recreation complex that includes a golf course, snack bar, ballroom facilities and tennis courts. A combination of six clay courts and two hard courts are ready for any and all types of play. Belmont now serves as the home for several league teams, and the courts stay consistently full in the evenings and on weekends.

The granddaddy of the public parks, however, is none other than Byrd Park. Byrd Park has been around since 1907. During that time there isn't anything it has not seen. In May 1968, the Davis Cup tie between the USA and The Caribbean/West Indies teams was played at Byrd Park. USA team members included Stan Smith, Bob Lutz, Clark Graebner and Arthur Ashe. The U. S. won 5 to 0.

The Richmond City Tennis Championships, currently called The Davenport Richmond City Tennis Championships, are held there every year. "The Davenport," as it is called, consists of the junior singles, junior doubles, men's open singles and doubles, women's open singles and doubles and the mixed doubles open. Virtually every "name" player from the Richmond area has played in the city tournament. The list is lengthy and includes pro circuit players, satellite players and a huge number of college players.

Byrd Park was the site of the Home Beneficial Tennis Tournament. The "Home Benny" was a very strong junior tournament sponsored by Home Beneficial Life Insurance Company and was a tune-up for sectional and national tournaments. The Jaycees Tournament was another summer event for juniors, a stepping stone tournament for competitive players yet to win a title.

If Byrd Park is the granddaddy of public facilities, then Sam Woods is the granddaddy of the public courts. For nearly twenty years, he influenced the lives of many young players through their mutual love of tennis. Many of Sam's students could not afford tennis lessons, so he taught them for free, as well as strung their rackets. Mr. Woods lobbied for college scholarships on behalf of his kids, who otherwise would not have attended college. Same also turned out more than his share of great tennis players. O. H. Parrish, Bobby Boertner, Bobby Payne, Del Sylvia, Bruce Sylvia and Lanny Ross are just a few who went on to play college tennis, with some winning state and national championships.

Clubs

By Tom Hood

Some people come to Richmond to visit and some come to stay. You never know. Those that stay seek relaxation and it is a good bet they find it on the tennis courts at any one of the clubs in one of the best tennis towns in America! The clubs come in all sizes so for the sake of simplicity let's put them in one of two categories: country clubs and major racket clubs.

Country clubs are the big boys. They've got it all: swimming pool(s), golf course(s), dining room(s) and tennis courts.

The Country Club of Virginia has been around the longest and has more tennis history than the others so it leads the way in the country club category. CCV first opened its doors in 1908. The facility has grown to where it now has twenty-four tennis courts. During the post-WWII years the tennis scene was dominated by Bobby Leitch and Al Dickinson. Fred Koechlein became the pro in 1959 and he stayed until 1974. During Fred's tenure, tennis activity at the club expanded and so did the list of talented players including Bitsy Harrison, Sarah Townsend, Shelton Horsley, O.H. Parrish, Amanda Macauley, Bill Correll and Lindsay Burn. Chris Blair, Rob Leitch, John Leitch, Stuart Horsley, Garrett Horsley, Bobby Fauntleroy, Betty Baugh Harrison and Lloyd Hatcher helped round out the highly ranked talent that got started during that era. Former U.S. Davis Cup player Harold (Hal) Burrows followed Fred, and Tom Wallace took over in 1998. The program multiple national champion Julie Kaczmarek Ogborne and former touring pro Carl Clark, with Rob Oaks and Scott Mitchell rounding out the teaching duties. The Country Club of Virginia has hosted a wide variety of tournaments and events over the years. To name just a few, CCV was home to the Richmond City Tennis Tournament for several decades, held the Virginia State Indoor Championships from 1996-2010, an exhibition between grand slam champions Bobby Riggs and Don Budge, and the club was the venue for Bill Tilden's National Professional Clay Court Championships featuring Bill Tilden and Fred Perry.

Willow Oaks Country Club is one of the oldest country clubs in Richmond. Willow Oaks offers twelve tennis courts. Steve Leovey was one of its earliest pros and was there many years. Leovey produced a strong group of players who competed for state titles in the junior divisions including Drew Gallilee, Chip King, Ron Weisinger, Herb Weisinger and Buck Ward. During Leovey's time, Willow Oaks hosted one of the strongest junior tournaments in the city. Even though it did not bring in a lot of out-of-towners, it was still an honor to win. Former VCU coach Bill Doeg, Tom Magner, Fred Koechlein and Lynn Bybee all put their mark on Willow Oaks as head pros. Cris Robinson leads a new charge for the club today. Cris, who played No. 1 for Clemson and was a national clay court champion himself, has brought in world class talent such as Mike Ciszek. Melissa Robinson, Andres Amores and Laura Tuchscherer not only teach the usual clinics and private lessons but put on a vast array of programs. These programs include junior-targeted events like Tennis Night in America and QuickStart Tennis tournaments, as well as tennis exhibitions featuring former touring pros. Willow Oaks also hosts workshops for tournament directors, college coaches and high school coaches, as well as the Davenport City Senior Championships.

Willow Oaks hosted a celebrity Pro-Am fundraiser in March 2011 to benefit the RTA and Virginia Heroes.

Salisbury Country Club was built in the Salisbury subdivision on the south side of Richmond. The original tennis facility consisted of two hard courts, four soft courts lining Salisbury Road and a small pro shop. Wayne Tucker was the first pro, and despite the modest tennis facility, Wayne enjoyed a solid core of tennis enthusiasts. Jack Cummings took over after Wayne and both Jack and the club had pretty impressive runs. Salisbury later added a three-court indoor tennis facility. Jack was the head pro during those expansion years and also coached his daughter Kathleen Cummings (see Hall of Famers chapter). Jack's entire family was active in tennis. His wife, LeLe, played and helped out at the club; his oldest daughter Peggy ran tournaments for the Virginia Slims women's pro tour. His youngest daughter Mary played tournaments as a junior, and his son played high school tennis and taught tennis for several years. Playing out of Salisbury, Tom Hood, Cal Cromer, Kyle Woolfolk and Frank DePew along with other clubs' Larry Hudson, Becky Nierle, Judy Keith and Mark Warlick, led the way to the district title in 1973 for Midlothian High School. The dynasty really began in 1976 when Salisbury's John DePew, Greg Miller and Rob Pinkham made up half of the team that won an incredible five consecutive state championships for Midlothian High School.

Salisbury Country Club recently added a viewing deck for the McDonald's Mid-Atlantic Clay Court Championships.

Today Scott Steinour runs the show as Salisbury's Director of Tennis. While he, J. T. Murphy and Sandi Rosato have put together a fine overall program, the tennis world in Richmond turns its attention to Salisbury Country Club the second and third weeks of July for the McDonald's Mid-Atlantic Clay Court Championships. Scott, along with Bill Barnes, has put together the premier tennis tournament in the area. The "McDonald's Clay Courts" consists of men's and women's singles, doubles and mixed doubles. The tournament features current and former world-ranked players along with some of the best collegians in the country. The quality of tennis is so high that people come from miles away to watch the matches. Scott and Bill have created the perfect combination of an enjoyable social event with the best tennis in town.

Hermitage Country Club used to call Hilliard Road in Richmond home but moved to Goochland County in 1973. Hermitage's tennis program is on the move as well. Tennis pro Mark Bernstine, former Virginia Tech tennis star, and his dedicated group of players hosted the senior tour featuring Jimmy Connors and John McEnroe in the late 1990s and Hermitage became the center of the tennis universe for a while. An instant increase in tennis interest was felt throughout the club and more people began to play. The club capitalized on the surge by building a state-of-the-art indoor tennis facility in 2005. The club recently co-hosted a national level 16 and under tournament featuring some of the top juniors in the country. Hermitage is not without its stars. Martha Beddingfield, arguably one of the finest women tennis players from Richmond, won the high school state championships, was a two-time All-American and a member of the University of Richmond's national championship team. Craig Dawson won the all armed forces tournament in 1978.

Stonehenge Golf and Country Club has been around for a long time as well and has six hard courts. Chris Sutmiller runs the show there now as the head pro. Stonehenge at one time hosted an open tournament just before the Virginia State Tennis Championships. Many of the top players used it as a tune up for the "State" tournament similar to the way the pros use the Queens Cup tournament as a tune up for Wimbledon. It must have worked! Jimmy Milley played in it and won the State Open three consecutive years. Tony Velo played in it and was a finalist at the State Open. Stonehenge also hosted the state 35 and over hard courts for several years and showcased some incredible matches between Bill Doeg, Brian Clark and former touring pro Graham Stilwell. Brian Clark beat Bill Doeg 7-6, 6-7, 7-6 in a marathon quarterfinal match and followed it up later that day with an upset win over Stilwell in the semifinals. Exhausted from the win, Clark had little left for the final, which Wake Forest standout Chris Blair won in straight sets.

The Dominion Club can not only boast at having former city champion Joe Cappellino running the show as Director of Tennis but also has former womens city champion Keri Nimitz as an active member. Along with other top flighted players such as Tom Bryan, Andy Todd, Rich

Razzetti (University of Richmond Hall of Famer) and Chapin Jones, the Dominion Club has an impressive core of tennis enthusiasts. With five clay courts and four hard courts, the Dominion Club can accommodate any style of play. Cappellino along with head pro Danny Fariss engage in an active junior program and host several junior tournaments throughout the summer.

Jefferson Lakeside Country Club has multiple city and Middle Atlantic Doubles champion Tom Magner at the helm, and Meadowbrook Country Club just acquired Chris Radtke. Lastly, none can dispute the credentials of Richmond Country Club's Jamie Hevron. Jamie played No. 1 for Virginia Commonwealth University and has won both city and state championships on multiple occasions as one of the area's premier competitors.

Major racquet clubs are basically country clubs without a golf course. Like the country clubs, they come in all sizes.

The Westwood Club leads the way here. There isn't much Westwood has not done. From its earliest years it has been home to city champions like Joe Kranitsky (doubles 1947) and Frank Hartz (singles 1948, doubles 1948). In 1966, Eddie Phillips took the title in both singles and doubles with partner Dick Makepeace. Makepeace took the doubles title again in 1967. Richard McKee, son of Westwood pro Dick McKee, took home the city trophy in 1970 at the ripe old age of seventeen. In 1970, Hugh Waters took over the reins and brought with him some more tennis talent. In 1973, Westwood teaching pro Tom Magner won the first of his three Thalhimers city titles. Magner defeated fellow Westwood member Neal Carl in the city finals in 1974. Mark Vines, now a Westwood member, stood in the winner's circle in 1975. A dry spell hit until 1993 when 18-year-old David Caldwell took the crown. In 1996, Westwood head pro Sean Steinour won the first of his record-breaking 8 city championships. On the women's side, even though the list isn't quite as long, the quality is unmatched. Future touring pro Flo Bryan, one of the top women players ever to come from Richmond, won three consecutive titles from 1972 to 1974. As a member of the Westwood family, Rachel Gale won one of her four titles in 2003, and Lindsey Wyeth won her city singles crown in 2004.

The Westwood Club has played host to any number of tournaments and events. The professional women's tour stopped here in 1970 and ran through 1973 featuring Billie Jean King and Rosie Casals. Westwood held pro senior events as well. For years the State 35 and over championships were held on Westwood's clay courts. One of the most popular tournaments was the Ralph Whitaker Doubles Tournament held each January featuring some of the best tennis to watch. Colleges used the "Ralph Whitaker" as a tune up tournament and so they sent their best tennis teams to get ready for the upcoming season. With such talent coming to town, it was not unusual to see the occasional touring pro, such as Charlie Owens, make an appearance.

While Romain Ambert, Lindsey Wyeth, Amy Noland and Miguel Castro handle the tennis duties, Westwood continues to be a tennis force today as host of the Anthem Challenge. Held in late September, the "Anthem" is the largest tennis event in the city. Over 700 players of all levels, each representing their respective clubs, compete in a friendly team competition. The team with the most points at the end of the three-day event takes home the Anthem Cup and bragging rights for a year.

A handful of visionaries headed by Jack Keith decided it was time for a major swim and racquet facility south of the James River and Briarwood Swim and Racquet Club was born in the late 60s. A state-of-the-art facility for its time, it had 3 indoor clay courts, 11 outdoor clay courts and 3 outdoor hard courts. It also had something no other facility had at the time, a stadium court. Ralph Flora was the first pro at Briarwood, and he was one of the first to offer year-round tennis practices for juniors venturing into the tournament world. Briarwood was host to the Virginia State  Tennis Championships for several years. Other state and sectional tournaments have been played there over the years such as the Virginia State Clay Courts. The club has gone through a number of changes over the years and is now called ACAC. Jason Kinder, Rachel Gale, Bruce Sibling and Ben Zaiser lead an active program that includes some top-ranked juniors including Bryce DePew and Liam Sullivan. ACAC tennis pros and members are also known for fielding very competitive USTA league teams.

Raintree Swim and Racquet Club — just the name is synonymous with Richmond tennis. Not quite as old as some of the other clubs, the important role Raintree has played in the local tennis community during its time is unrivaled. The doors opened in 1974 with Robert Cucci as the pro. The club was a unique facility with four indoor hard courts, eight outdoor courts, a snack bar, a pool, social area and offices all overlooking Raintree lake in the West End of town. Fred Koechline followed Cucci. In 1977, the club went up for sale and Hugh Waters, seeing the opportunity to own his own club, seized it. Fully armed with his own major facility and his own imagination Hugh and Raintree took off. Known as the Friendly Club, that is exactly what Raintree became, the friendly club to all levels of play. Former city champion Tom Magner came over from Willow Oaks to be head teaching pro. Future women's VCU coach and teaching pro Eva Bard added her talents as well. There was no limit to all the tennis activity taking place at Raintree. The Virginia State Open became the tournament to play, and top players came from all over the state. Players such as UNC All-American Billy Brock came, touring pro John Hill came from Norfolk, Mike Eikenberry came from Charlottesville, four-time champion Bobby Heald came from Lynchburg, three-time champion Jimmy Milley came from Danville and former Wimbledon quarterfinalist Gene Russo came from northern Virginia. The women saw Margaret Russo from Northern Virginia and touring pro Leigh Thompson from Newport News. These

players along with Richmond's own incredible talent put on some of the best tennis to be seen. The atmosphere was social as well so the event became a great place to play, watch and enjoy the great game of tennis.

Some of the other great activities Hugh and the Raintree team put together were the qualifying tournament and official practice facility for the UVB Tennis Classic, the Ginny women's pro tournament, competitive USTA league teams and a practice environment for many of the city's top players. Even the member-guest tournaments were full. The office space was converted to an aerobics and fitness center and a whole new clientele joined.

Perhaps the best thing to come out of Raintree was its junior program. Hundreds of kids were introduced to tennis and many of them went on to compete in junior tournaments, high school, collegiate and even pro levels. Raintree's junior program became the feed for the Mills Godwin High School boys and girls tennis teams.

In 1987 Hugh sold to East West Partners and Mark Vines and Buzz Frye each spent time as the head pros. In 1989 East West's John Hill brought in Eddie Parker to run the show and in 1998 Eddie, along with his father Marshall Parker, fulfilled a dream and bought the club from East West and together they ran the club for the next decade. Marshall retired in 2009, leaving Eddie and his wife Stacey to continue the tennis excellence at Raintree. The Virginia State Open is gone but Raintree recently hosted a national 16s tournament with some of the top players from all over the country. The Parkers, along with Phil Thacker, Ricardo Ribera and Tatsiana Uvarova, insure the junior program thrives as Raintree continues to feed both Mills Godwin and Deep Run High Schools' state championship teams.

For years, Burkwood Swim and Racquet Club was a very nice community association in Hanover County. Slowly things began to change. The progressive thinking started when Jim Shakespeare and the tennis committee decided to open up the member-guest tournament to anyone, something that was not typically done at that time. The draw was filled with a who's who of Richmond players who had won city, state, sectional and even national tournaments including Tom Magner, Ward Hamilton, Jim Milley, Jim Shakespeare and Rusty Whitaker. Plans were made for Burkwood to aggressively expand its tennis facility, and it was the first recreation association to open its doors to four indoor tennis courts. Former Virginia Tech tennis stars Ed Butterworth and Leslie Seward Butterworth direct tennis operations at this premier facility. Burkwood boasts an active presence in USTA league play and a rising junior program with Audrey Butterworth leading the way.

Courtside West, another West End tennis facility that opened in 1978, offers three indoor courts, two racquetball courts, and office space to rent. Jim Shakespeare called Courtside West home for many years. Now former UVA star and two-time city champion Damian Sancilio is the man. Damian and John Shipstedt emphasize a hard work ethic with the juniors and have created a junior workout program where some of Richmond's top juniors fine-tune their games.

Midlothian Athletic Club, formerly Robious Sports and Fitness Club, has 2 indoor tennis courts and 9 outdoor courts, 2 of which are covered with a bubble during the winter. Al Thomas is the head pro and has a very strong contingent of USTA league teams. Midlothian Athletic Club is known to show well in the Anthem Challenge.

Woodlake Swim and Racquet Club has one of the best doubles players around as its head pro in Ken McKay. Located in the Woodlake subdivision in Chesterfield County, the club has 16 clay courts and Ken and company have some of the strongest league teams in the city. Woodlake is also very active in junior development.

Midlothian Tennis Club is fairly new but has been around for a while, all at the same time. Brandermill Country Club was part of the planned community movement of the late 1960s and early 70s. Former University of Richmond tennis star Dave Snidow was one of the earliest pros there along with John DePew, Darryl Wilburn, John Hill and Rachel Gale. Tennis was vibrant during those years at Brandermill, producing such top ranked players as Kristin Lanio and state open champion Norm Schellenger, Jr. Things began to slip, however, as players moved to other clubs or other sports. A core group of die-hard tennis enthusiasts decided to do something about it. They purchased the courts and built a four-court indoor facility which opened in 2010. The name of the club was changed to Midlothian Tennis Club. Former VCU standout and nationally acclaimed teaching pro Feisal Hassan was hired in early 2012 as Director of Tennis and things are on the move up for this young and old facility.

Recreation Associations

Sometime during the first half of this century John Q. Suburbia met John Q. Public and took a whole chunk of the population with it. People turned their attention to the outskirts of town and beyond in order to get a little more elbow room and the suburbs were born. In many of these new subdivisions, developers built places where people could meet and socialize called community or recreation associations. These "rec" associations offered an affordable alternative to the more expensive clubs. Each recreation association offered its own set of amenities but all of them had two things: a swimming pool and a tennis court. A whole new population was introduced to tennis. True to the theory of unexpected consequences, a remarkable thing began to happen; many of these tennis-playing youngsters actually began to like the sport. The "rec" kids entered tournaments and caused local tournament draws to swell. It was not long before these kids were not only competitive but taking home trophies. From these little old community associations came some of the best tennis players the city has ever seen! It wasn't just the youngsters that caught the tennis bug; moms and dads did too. Friday night tennis socials, ladder matches, league matches, club championships and member-guest tennis tournaments all added to an enjoyable social atmosphere.

Avalon Recreation Association is located on Heathfield Road, off Derbyshire Road in Richmond's West End and has eight tennis courts. Avalon is one of the few recreation associations fortunate to have a year-round pro in the name of Charlie Palmer. Charlie keeps things happening with vibrant junior programs, including QuickStart Tennis clinics and an active adult program. Many of Charlie's protégés are competitive in local tournaments. Avalon is also a participant in the annual Autumn Cup competition. It has been regarded as one of the top recreation associations in Henrico County for many years.

Kanawha Recreation Association is another top-notch community association that is home to an amazing four pools and nine tennis courts. Kanawha has Matt Magner as its lead pro but the program is strong enough to have Whitt Sheppard and Del Moser help with teaching duties. Kanawha is another competitor in the Autumn Cup. Arguably one of the top five women to play in Richmond, Sharon Dunsing, cut her tennis teeth at Kanawha. Sharon was a member of the University of Richmond tennis team that won a national championship and later won back-to-back women's singles titles at the city tournament in 1986 and 1987.

Southampton Recreation Association is located just off Cherokee Road on Chellow Road and has greatly upgraded its tennis program with the addition of tennis pro Lynn Bybee. Lynn's resume is quite impressive. Along with twenty-five years of teaching experience, Lynn is a very accomplished player. Quite competitive on the national level, Lynn has been ranked as high as fourth in the nation and won a national doubles title in his age division. Southampton was one of the teams to beat from the 1970s in the old Suburban Tennis League when former University of Richmond tennis player and age group city doubles champion Larry Rauppius was on the team. Lynn has Southampton charging forward and is now another one of the growing number of Autumn Cup participants. Southampton is very unique and truly a year-round recreation facility, it being the only one with an indoor skating rink.

Ridgetop Recreation Association is tucked away on Ridgetop Road, just off Patterson Avenue in Henrico County. With five courts, full time pro Pat Anderson manages to offer a complete tennis program. Heavily active with the juniors, Pat also has a strong adult team as they just captured the 2011 Autumn Cup.

Canterbury and Chestnut Oaks historically have been two of the stronger recreation associations. Canterbury, located on Pump Road in the West End, is a multi-court facility that includes junior standouts Thad and Tim Polk as two of its alumni. Today Gonzalo Garcia is Canterbury's head pro and he offers a variety of spring, summer and fall programs. Chestnut Oaks Recreation Association is located on Parham Road, and Sandy Hinchman is the summer instructor there. Chestnut Oaks alumni tennis stars include Debbie Brooks and Kim Eubank.

Twin Hickory, King's Charter, Woodmont, The Colonies and Wyndham each have their own community associations and promote tennis with their own summer programs.

Each recreation association may argue the merits of its own club but over the years it is hard to deny the storied success of the next two.

Three Chopt Recreation Association. The success of a club can partially be measured by the success of its alumni and few rival that of Three Chopt. Bob Hardy, Jim Craven, Lila Gilliam and Gary Burton created an atmosphere that encouraged junior play. Lila helped create the Bantam (junior) League. They all encouraged including juniors with adult tennis playing whenever possible. The results were five incredibly talented tennis players. Irving Cantor was not only a top-ranked junior; he went on to play at UVA. John Tate was one of the top high school players in the area. Steve Gilliam was one of the top two juniors for his age group and went on to play in the

top three at the University of Kentucky. Brian Clark ended up at Virginia Tech where he played between #2 and #4 for the team. While playing #4 he set a school record for most matches won in one year. Last is Mark Vines. Mark's tennis accomplishments have been so impressive that in 2009 he was inducted in the Richmond Tennis Hall of Fame.

Today Rob Johnston, Three Chopt's teaching pro, is using his fifteen years of experience to push the club to new heights. Rob's junior program and camps are such that he needs two assistants, Jeff Wheeler and Tom Young, to help out. This year for the first time Three Chopt had a mixed 7.5 team advance to the district championships following an undefeated regular season. Back in 1977, Three Chopt's Kaki Vint, along with Raintree's Ginger Cuthbert, started the Richmond Ladies Primetime Tennis League. The league targeted women of all levels over the age of 40 wanting to play social tennis. Unique from the Suburban League, players came from other clubs as well as non-club members. The league started with 10 teams, but, thanks to Kaki's and Ginger's vision and assistance from people like Shelley Stepp, the league now boasts over 30 teams divided into 4 sections.

Bon Air Community Association. Doors first opened for Bon Air around the late 1950s with one small swimming pool, an asphalt tennis court and dirt banking as the spectator section. John Wray took Bon Air under his wing, and the club expanded by adding two more courts, another swimming pool and a club house. Eventually, lights were added to the existing three courts and six more courts were built under Wray's watchful eye, for whom the courts are named. More importantly than the physical structures was the attitude toward tennis that was fostered. Mr. Wray, along with John Rose, Dick Blanton, Jack Cummings and Randy Blunt, created an encouraging atmosphere for youth and adult tennis.

The youth program was enhanced by bantam league play and junior tournaments. Juniors at Bon Air were encouraged to play in open tournaments at other clubs as well. Summer instructors such as Chuck Gordon, Matt Maddox, John McGinty and Bon Air's own Greg Williams were hired not only for their playing ability but for their ability to interact with the juniors as well. The upshot was Bon Air always had tons of "young-uns" on the tennis courts.

The result of all this feel good tennis was something quite incredible. First, Bon Air had two women's teams and four men's teams playing suburban league. Starting in 1974, the top men's team with the likes of Walker Richardson, Dan Richardson, John Wray, Jack Cummings, Coleman Ticer, Tim Tinsley, Bill Barnard and Jim Robertson won the coveted Suburban Saturday morning league team championship, beating out some of the top teams in the city.

Bon Air was one of the first recreation associations to incorporate juniors into adult programs, like the club championships. This approach encouraged juniors to keep playing, and the excellent job done by those early summer pros produced some remarkable results, especially for a recreation association. In 1979, eleven players in the juniors from Bon Air held state rankings with three of them being ranked No. 1! Keith Geisler and Stephanie Hiedeman were ranked in the 12s, Catherine Greer and Amy Dickerson in the 14s and Kathleen Cummings was No. 1 in girls 18s. On the boys' side, Barney Wilson was ranked in the 16s, Jeff Jones, Hal Greer and Doug Wilburn were ranked in the 18s, Darryl Wilburn was ranked No. 1 in the boys 16s and Steve Wilson was ranked No. 1 in the boys 18s. Wilburn went on to star on the men's team at UVA and claim both city and state titles during the 80s. Steve, Jeff, Barney and Hal were all part of the Midlothian High School tennis team that won five consecutive state championships. Three of Bon Air's alumni went on to obtain world rankings. Not bad for a community association!

Arenas

By Tom Hood

Where were all the tourneys played, long time passing? Back in the day when each sport had its defined season, tennis was strictly a summer activity. Sometime around late May the rackets were dusted off, and put back after the Labor Day tournaments were completed. When Lou Einwick decided to invite a few of the best players in the world to town for a little tournament, a venue had to be found.

First stop, the Arena. Built in 1908 as part of the Virginia State Fair, it was capable of holding nearly 5,000 people. The Arena was not very fancy, just a big old building next to the Diamond, and was used for everything from rock concerts to basketball games. It was, however, the largest facility in the city so in February of 1966 it provided the perfect venue for the first Fidelity Bankers Life Tennis Tournament. A tennis court was installed between the bleachers, an umpire's chair brought in and Richmond had its very own version of an indoor center court. Having such a high level tournament was something quite novel to Richmond so there was a definite buzz around town. The tournament was packed. The Fidelity tournament, later the United Virginia Bank Tennis Classic, stayed at the Arena until 1971 when it moved to greener pastures. The Arena had one last tennis hurrah in 1983 when it hosted the finals for what was billed as the "World's Largest Tennis Tournament." In 1990, the old boy had finally outlived its purpose, and it was torn down.

Tennis fans packed the Arena to enjoy an evening of professional tennis in March 1960. Pictured above are Alex Olmedo (near court) and Pancho Segura. *Courtesy of Richmond Times-Dispatch.*

In 1971 a state of the art facility was built smack dab in downtown Richmond, the Coliseum. This new venue seemed to have it all: multi-level viewing, individual cushioned seating and a capacity of up to 12,000 people. With the upgrade in facility came an upgrade in the annual UVB tournament. The draw was expanded to 32 players and prize money was increased. The Coliseum also had enhanced locker room facilities for the players. There were separate rooms on the bottom floor that could be used for tournament officials or set up as a VIP lounge. Multiple concession stands were available at each level so one could step out for popcorn, a corn dog and a soft drink, with hardly missing a double fault. Yes indeed! This new Coliseum was quite the facility for enjoying a lively tennis match. The Fidelity/UVB was not the only tennis being played at the Coliseum. In 1982 an exhibition was played between

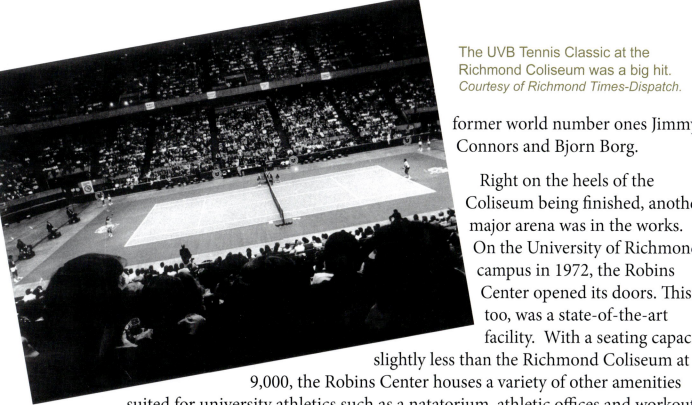

The UVB Tennis Classic at the Richmond Coliseum was a big hit. *Courtesy of Richmond Times-Dispatch.*

former world number ones Jimmy Connors and Bjorn Borg.

Right on the heels of the Coliseum being finished, another major arena was in the works. On the University of Richmond campus in 1972, the Robins Center opened its doors. This, too, was a state-of-the-art facility. With a seating capacity slightly less than the Richmond Coliseum at 9,000, the Robins Center houses a variety of other amenities suited for university athletics such as a natatorium, athletic offices and workout rooms. The Robins Center is also an excellent venue for tennis. It was site of the Central Fidelity Banks International women's pro tournament which featured the top women in the world such as Martina Navratilova and Tracy Austin. In 1983, the Richmond Coliseum was already booked so the scheduled UVB men's tournament was moved to the Robins Center. The Robins Center was also home to a special event featuring a series of legends matches held between former women tennis greats including Martina Navratilova, Evonne Goolagong and Virginia Wade.

The Arthur Ashe, Jr. Athletic Center, located on the Boulevard next to the Diamond, is a venue capable of hosting a variety of sports activities. The Ashe Center once hosted the Intercollegiate Tennis Association's National Indoor Championships. In recent years it has been the site of junior-related programs and activities such as QuickStart Tennis and Tennis Night in America festivities. On March 24, 2011, at the Ashe Center, Mayor Dwight Jones recognized the RTA and the City of Richmond for its promotion of community tennis, declaring it "Tennis Night in Richmond."

The Siegel Center was finished in May of 1999 and is a multi-use arena on the VCU campus in downtown Richmond. Capable of seating upwards of 7,500 warm bodies, it is ideal for basketball, graduations, concerts and, of course, tennis. In 2001, the Trigon Champions senior tour made a stop at the Siegel Center. Numerous tennis exhibitions have been played there and have included former world number ones Andre Agassi, Stefanie Graf, Serena Williams, Andy Roddick, Lindsay Davenport and Jennifer Capriati.

CHAPTER 4

EVENTS

The City Tournament

By John Packett

The Richmond City Tennis Championships have a lengthy and distinguished history as one of the best and toughest tournaments in Virginia.

Many of the state's top players have reigned as champions in both the men's and women's divisions, and some went on to greater glory on the professional circuits.

> "The city tournament is what it is. It's been around forever, it seems, and is a great opportunity to showcase Richmond tennis."
> — Sean Steinour

Two of the best-known female players are Margaret Anderson Duval, who won more titles in that category (seven) than any other woman, and Kathleen Cummings, who won back-to-back crowns in the mid-1970s before performing well on the pro tour.

Duval was the younger sister of Penelope Anderson McBride, who was an excellent player in her own right, reaching the singles quarterfinals of the U.S. Nationals on five occasions and playing in the French championships and Wimbledon. She was also a member of the Wightman Cup team.

"She was very steady," two-time city runner-up Betty Gustafson said of Margaret Duval. "Her strokes were not hard but well-placed. I played doubles with her. She had the kind of game where she never gave up."

Duval won the last of her singles titles in 1951. Gustafson was runner-up in 1965 and '67.

Charles Thalhimer presenting trophy to 1975 city champion Mark Vines. Courtesy of Richmond Times-Dispatch.

Cummings captured her first city championship at 14, becoming the youngest ever at the time to accomplish it. Her record was later surpassed by Leanne Seward. Cummings was ranked as high as 48th in the world on the women's tour.

On the men's side, Bitsy Harrison, Mark Vines, Tom Cain, Junie Chatman, and Wade McGuire made some inroads on the men's circuit after winning the city title. McGuire was the youngest (16) to claim the men's crown.

Rachel Gale has won over a dozen city titles in singles, doubles and mixed doubles.

Chatman is the only African-American player to win the city tournament, doing it twice. Arthur Ashe was not allowed to play in the city tourney because blacks were not welcome at the Country Club of Virginia and Byrd Park in those segregated days of the 1950s and early 60s.

The first African-American female to reach the final was Koren Fleming in 2005, and she lost to Rachel Gale.

Gale, who played No. 1 singles for Virginia Commonwealth University and is a native of Rochester, NY, captured the second-most singles championships among the women with six, the last of which came in 2006.

"It's the most near and dear tournament to my heart," said Gale. "The first year [1992] I played in it, I lost to Valerie Farmer in the final. The next year, my father had passed away, and I told him I was playing for him."

"The next tournament [after he died] was the city tournament, and I won all three events [singles, doubles and mixed].

"Of course, I kept playing the tournament every year because it reminded me of my father and winning all three titles. The last time I won all three was in 2006, and that's when I stopped playing in that tournament."

"I wanted to go out for my dad, having won all three that year. That's how I started and that's how I ended it."

Gale said she enjoyed the competition, which was tougher during her time than it has been in recent years with smaller draws.

"That's what made it fun and exciting," said Gale, a teaching pro for many years in the area. "I looked forward to it. I wanted the hard first round because I wanted to be ready if I made it to the final. It was a good run."

The most prolific winner among the men is Sean Steinour, who captured eight singles titles from 1996 through 2007. The New Jersey native could have won more, finishing as the runner-up on four occasions, the last in 2008.

"I'm a competitive person, and I always like playing tournaments," said Steinour, who was head pro at the Westwood Club for over 15 years. "The city tournament is what it is. It's been around forever, it seems, and is a great opportunity to showcase Richmond tennis."

"Of course, I wanted to support the [co-sponsoring] Richmond Tennis Association, which I've always done in many different ways. It's a fun opportunity to compete, and it's right here in Richmond. I feel like I'm representing Westwood and that's a big deal in itself."

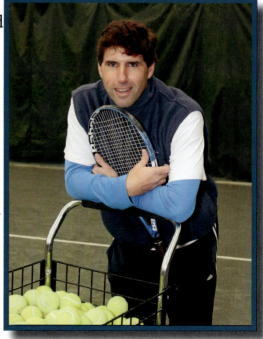

Eight-time champion Sean Steinour

"I'm excited to be in the history books, so to speak. It's really cool. I can tell my kids about it when they're old enough to understand."

In the early days, the tournament was held at the Country Club of Virginia, when tennis was more of a country-club sport. It moved to Byrd Park in the late 1960s and, except for the 2005 city tournament that was played on the clay courts at Briarwood, has remained there ever since under different sponsorships, most recently Davenport and Company.

Other well-known champions over the years were Bobby Leitch (five-time winner), Del Sylvia, Bruce Sylvia (four-time winner), O.H. Parrish (four-time winner), Cliff Miller (six-time winner), Carl Clark, Tom Magner, Jay Bruner, Lindsay Wortham, Ginny Wortham, Amanda Macaulay, Sarah Harrison (four-time winner), Flo Bryan and Bridget Reichert (five-time winner).

In the May 24, 1958 edition of the *Richmond Times-Dispatch*, the Thalhimer family was cited for their support of the growth of tennis in Richmond. They were early patrons of tennis in Richmond and sponsored the City Tournament for many years. In this photograph, daughter Barbara and father William Thalhimer, Jr. (left) play son Billy and mom Barbara, while youngest son Bobby observes. *Photo courtesy of the William G. Thalhimer, III archive.*

RICHMOND CITY T

Year	Men's Singles Champion	Women's Singles Champion
1947	Bobby Leitch	Mrs. Ann Whipple
1948	Frank Hartz	Mrs. Ed Hudgins
1949	Henry Valentine	Margaret Anderson
1950	Shelton Horsley	Mrs. Polk Neal
1951	Del Sylvia	Margaret Anderson
1952	Del Sylvia	Mrs. Marge Lundlin
1953	Bobby Payne	Mrs. Jane Gee
1954	Del Sylvia	Ann Whitfield
1955	Gene Wash	Carol Dickerson
1956	Chuck Straley	Mrs. James Russ
1957	Bobby Payne	Frances White
1958	Bobby Bortner	Amanda Tevepaugh
1959	Bobby Bortner	Amanda Tevepaugh
1960	Bitsy Harrison	Betty Pierotti
1961	Bruce Sylvia	Amanda Tevepaugh
1962	O.H. Parrish	Sarah Townsend
1963	Bruce Sylvia	Mrs. James Russ
1964	Bruce Sylvia	Sarah Townsend
1965	O.H. Parrish	Sarah Townsend
1966	Eddie Phillips	Lee Price
1967	O.H. Parrish	Marietta McCarty
1968	Bruce Sylvia	Sarah Townsend
1969	O.H. Parrish	Sue Cain
1970	Richard McKee	Lindsay Burn
1971	Mike Eikenberry	Lindsay Burn
1972	Mike Eikenberry	Flo Bryan
1973	Tom Magner	Flo Bryan
1974	Tom Magner	Flo Bryan
1975	Mark Vines	Betty Baugh Harrison
1976	Tom Cain	Kathleen Cummings
1977	Tom Cain	Kathleen Cummings
1978	Junie Chatman	Leanne Seward

TENNIS CHAMPIONS

Year	Men's Singles Champion	Women's Singles Champion
1979	Tom Magner	Leanne Seward
1980	Pat Perrin	Leanne Seward
1981	Darryl Wilburn	Lindsay B. Wortham
1982	Darryl Wilburn	Maryse Hotchkiss
1983	Hugh Waters IV	Diane Sancilio
1984	Damian Sancilio	Diane Sancilio
1985	Junie Chatman	Martha Puryear
1986	Wade McGuire	Sharon Dunsing
1987	Mark Vines	Sharon Dunsing
1988	Norm Schellenger	Keri Nimitz
1989	Jamie Hevron	Martha Puryear
1990	Mark Vines	Martha Puryear
1991	Johan Dysholm	Valerie Farmer
1992	Jamie Hevron	Valerie Farmer
1993	David Caldwell	Rachel Gale
1994	Ed Butterworth	Kirsten Elim
1995	Joe Cappellino	Ivi Moorlat
1996	Sean Steinour	Shannon Cubitt
1997	Sean Steinour	Rachel Gale
1998	Sean Steinour	Rachel Gale
1999	Carl Clark	Julie Kaczmarek
2000	Jay Bruner	Bridget Bruner
2001	Jay Bruner	Bridget Bruner
2002	Sean Steinour	Chrissie Seredni
2003	Sean Steinour	Rachel Gale
2004	Sean Steinour	Lindsey Wyeth
2005	Sean Steinour	Rachel Gale
2006	Damian Sancilio	Rachel Gale
2007	Sean Steinour	Bridget B. Reichert
2008	Carl Clark	Bridget B. Reichert
2009	Martin Stiegwardt	Ginny Wortham
2010	Michal Ciszek	Ginny Wortham
2011	Matt Waddell	Bridget B. Reichert

Virginia State Tennis Championships

By John Packett

The Virginia State Tennis Championships have long been associated with the city of Richmond, and the area has produced many of its men's and women's champions through the years.

Until it left Richmond following the 2008 tournament, the state championships were held at the Country Club of Virginia, Briarwood Swim and Racquet Club (now ACAC) and Raintree Swim and Racquet Club.

The names of the men's and women's titlists read like a who's who of tennis in Richmond.

Among the local men's winners were O.H. Parrish, Bitsy Harrison, Bobby Bortner, Bruce Sylvia, Mark Vines, Junie Chatman, Darryl Wilburn and Norm Schellenger. On the women's side, winners included Kathleen Cummings, Diane Sancilio, Bridget Bruner Reichert and Lindsey Wyeth.

The state tournament enjoyed its longest run at Raintree, where it was held from 1974 until 2008.

Hugh Waters ran the tournament at Raintree during much of the 1970s and 80s, before Eddie Parker and his father, Marshall, bought the club in 1998. The Parkers were responsible for the State tourney through 2008.

"When we took it over in the 90s, we were able to get college players from different schools, Virginia Tech, Virginia, ODU," said Parker. "So a lot of the top college players were able to come and participate in the tournament along with most of the local pros.

"We got a lot of the [teaching] pros from the Northern Virginia area to come down and play, both on the men's and women's side."

The tournament didn't feature prize money for a number of years, but when pros became eligible to play in it, eventually there was cash involved, with the winners in each singles category receiving as much as $1,200.

Big crowds watched the action at Raintree.

"There was a lot of excitement. It was good for Raintree. It was good for Richmond. It was good for the state of Virginia to have a big-time, hard-court tournament," said Parker.

The men's and women's tournaments were held at the same site for the first time in 1977, when the women moved to Raintree with the men. Former touring pro Kim Shaefer of Great Falls was a five-time winner of the event at Raintree.

On the men's side, Bobby Heald was denied his fifth straight singles title when he experienced an upset stomach that contributed immensely to his five-set loss to Bill Shivar Jr., in the final at Briarwood in 1972.

The last player to win three in a row (1978-80) was Jim Milley of Danville who now lives in Richmond and was a former standout at Virginia Tech. He reached the final again in 1981 but was denied by Richmonder Mark Vines, a four-time winner himself.

"There were some very good players in it," said Milley. "As a matter of fact, I had no idea I was going to win it the first year I did in 1978. I had scheduled to go somewhere for another tournament that weekend because I figured I'd be out by then."

"The tournament was always during a very hot week [usually in early and mid-August]. I remember playing Adam Brock in the semis or quarterfinals one year and he cramped up [because of the heat] so bad he couldn't play."

For several years, the state tournament used block seeding because the draws were so big. That way, 16 players were seeded and the rest of the field played to them. It also gave the out-of-town teaching pros a few extra days at their clubs to give lessons.

Bobby Heald (left) and O. H. Parrish were top contenders for state titles throughout the 60s and into the 70s.

"That tournament was always so much fun because big Hugh [Waters] always did it up right," said Milley. "Made it a lot of fun."

When the draws began to shrink and it became more difficult to attract players, especially the pros, Parker had trouble finding sponsors. Eventually the money dried up altogether, and the decision was made to let the tournament go elsewhere.

"The last year or two, we ended up footing the bill a little bit, and the RTA actually helped out, just to keep it here," said Parker.

The State championships in Richmond have faded into the past now, and all that is left are memories of some hard-fought matches that lasted well into the evening and produced some of the best tennis ever seen in the city.

Virginia State Tennis Championships

Men's Singles Champions

1945 Jimmy Evert
1946 Hal Burrows
1948 Hal Burrows
1949 Shelton Horsley
1950 Shelton Horsley
1951 Del Sylvia
1952 Shelton Horsley
1953 Bobby Payne
1954 Del Sylvia
1955 Don Floyd
1956 Frank Spears
1957 Bobby Payne
1958 Bobby Payne
1959 King Lambert
1960 Bruce Sylvia
1961 Bruce Sylvia
1962 C.W. Shackleford
1963 O.H. Parrish
1964 Bob Bortner
1965 O.H. Parrish
1966 Bitsy Harrison
1967 O.H. Parrish
1968 Bobby Heald
1969 Bobby Heald
1970 Bobby Heald
1971 Bobby Heald
1972 Bill Shivar
1973 Billy Brock
1974 Billy Brock
1975 Bobby Heald
1976 Gene Russo
1977 Mark Vines
1978 Jim Milley
1979 Jim Milley
1980 Jim Milley
1981 Mark Vines
1982 Hugh Waters IV
1983 Junie Chatman
1984 Darryl Wilburn
1985 Norm Schellenger, Jr.
1986 Darryl Wilburn
1987 Mark Vines
1988 Norm Schellenger, Jr.
1989 Mark Vines
1990 Jamie Hevron
1991 Carl Clark
1992 Luciano D'Andrea
1993 Jamie Hevron
1994 Jamie Hevron
1995 Bear Schofield
1996 Sean Steinour
1997 Sean Steinour
1998 Daniel Colangelo
1999 Carl Clark
2000 Sean Steinour
2001 Trevor Spracklin
2002 Saber Kadiri
2003 Saber Kadiri
2004 Jose Bernard
2005 Somdev Devvarman
2006 Huntley Montgomery
2007 Brandon Corace
2008 Yakov Diskin

Women's Singles Champions

1959 Mary Slaughter	1985 Valerie Farmer
1960 Bonnie Loving	1986 Kim Shaefer
1961 Mary Slaughter	1987 Kim Shaefer
1962 Bonnie Loving	1988 Kim Shaefer
1963 Mary Slaughter	1989 Kim Shaefer
1964 Mary Slaughter	1990 Sylvia Schenck
1965 Sarah Townsend	1991 Kim Shaefer
1966 Sarah Townsend	1992 Michelle Dodds
1967 Adrian Price	1993 Jessica Steck
1968 Adrian Price	1994 Kirsten Elim
1969 Nancy Allen	1995 Karen VanderMerwe
1970 Nancy Allen	1996 Kirsten Elim
1971 Nancy Allen	1997 Rachel Gale
1972 Nancy Allen	1998 Jessica Steck
1974 Margaret Russo	1999 Martina Nedelkova
1975 Margaret Russo	2000 Sofia Hiort Wright
1976 Carole Ford	2001 Bridget Bruner
1977 Nancy Neviaser	2002 Nataly Cahana Fleishman
1978 Nancy Neviaser	2003 Lindsey Wyeth
1979 Kathleen Cummings	2004 Nataly Cahana Fleishman
1980 Leigh Anne Thompson	2005 Nataly Fleishman
1981 Amy Kneale	2006 Blakeley Griffith
1982 Amy Kneale	2007 Nataly Fleishman
1983 Diane Sancilio	2008 Viktoriya Konstantinova
1984 Valerie Farmer	

Jamie Hevron, a native Australian who starred for VCU in the mid 1980s, won the Virginia State Tennis Championship on three separate occasions.

Virginia State Indoor Championships

By Tom Hood

December is considered the happiest time of year so with everybody in such a jocular mood, the Country Club of Virginia decided to put on one of the toughest tournaments in the state, the Virginia State Indoor Championships, during that month. The event offered prize money totaling $10,000 so it attracted some of the best pros such as Carl Clark, Sean Steinour, Trevor Spracklin and Romain Ambert for the men, and Julie Kaczmarek Ogborne, Tatsiana Uvarova, Olga Borisova, Rachel Gale, Nataly Fleishman and Lindsey Howard for the women. Local college coaches Paul Kostin and Mark Wesselink saw the opportunity to get their players ready for the upcoming seasons so the field was strengthened by the addition of VCU's and the University of Richmond's tennis teams. Add a sprinkling of the best local high school players like Hunter Koontz, Anna Fuhr, Callie Whitlock and Max Schnur and a dash of the more competitive club players, and you have yourself a great tournament. The tournament ran from 1996 to 2010 and was a showcase for some truely extraordinary tennis.

In addition to being named tournament of the year in 1998 and 2002 by USTA/Virginia, the Virginia State Indoor Championships were considered very player-friendly for amenities such as a hospitality room to relax with food and drinks, a player party, excellent competition, full access to locker rooms and extensive gift bags. In other words, a first-class event.

2007 SMARTBOX Virginia State Indoor Women's Doubles champions Rachel Gale and Nataly Fleishman (pictured on the right) topped Kirsten Elim and Julie Ogborne 7-5, 6-1 in the finals.

Romain Ambert (left) defeated UVA's Rylan Rizza 6-3, 6-3 to win the 2006 SMARTBOX Virginia State Indoor title. Ambert won the men's singles title four years in a row (2006 - 2009).

"The indoor was one of the best organized and most welcoming tournaments. It had the best hospitality with a great laid back atmosphere despite the intense competition."
— Romain Ambert

2006 SMARTBOX Virginia State Indoor mixed doubles champions Carl Clark and Julie Ogborne (on the left) won the title by defeating Margie Walsh and Scott Steinour in the final.

Virginia State Indoor Champions

Year	Men's Singles Champion
1996	Sean Steinour
1997	Carl Clark
1998	Sean Steinour
1999	Sean Steinour
2000	John Winter
2001	Carl Clark
2002	Carl Clark
2003	Trevor Spracklin
2004	Pedro Nieto
2005	Marton Ott
2006	Romain Ambert
2007	Romain Ambert
2008	Romain Ambert
2009	Romain Ambert
2010	Thibaut Charron

Year	Men's Doubles Champions
1996	Fredrik Eliasson & Richard Wernerhjelm
1997	Carl Clark & Kurt Hammerscmidt
1998	Lee Harang & Trevor Spracklin
1999	Daniel Andersson & Richard Wernerhjelm
2000	Frank Moser & John Winter
2001	Carl Clark & Trevor Spracklin
2002	Carl Clark & Cris Robinson
2003	Carl Clark & Trevor Spracklin
2004	Daniel Andersson & Pedro Nieto
2005	Carl Clark & Trevor Spracklin
2006	Carl Clark & Trevor Spracklin
2007	Carl Clark & Trevor Spracklin
2008	Romain Ambert & Carl Clark
2009	Alexandru Cojanu & Juan Stiegwardt
2010	Thibaut Charron & Alexis Heugas

Year	Women's Singles Champion
1996	Ilona Poliakova
1997	Ly-Lan Schofield
1998	Rachel Gale
1999	Elyse Salahi
2000	Julie Kaczmarek
2001	Rachel Gale
2002	Lindsey Howard
2003	Bridget Merrick
2004	Nataly Fleishman
2005	Nataly Fleishman
2006	Ana Radeljevic
2007	Nataly Fleishman
2008	Tatsiana Uvarova
2009	Tatsiana Uvarova
2010	Tatsiana Uvarova

Year	Women's Doubles Champions
1996	Kirsten Elim & Julie Kaczmarek
1997	Lesia Bilak & Bridget Merrick
1998	Rachel Gale & Kim Shaefer
1999	Elizabeth Cascarilla & Janelle Williams
2000	Rachel Gale & Julie Kaczmarek
2001	Kirsten Elim & Julie Kaczmarek
2002	Rachel Gale & Julie Kaczmarek
2003	Bridget Merrick & Julie Kaczmarek
2004	Nataly Fleishman & Rachel Gale
2005	Nataly Fleishman & Rachel Gale
2006	Rachel Gale & Julie Kaczmarek
2007	Nataly Fleishman & Rachel Gale
2008	Olga Borisova & Viktoriya Konstantinova
2009	Olga Borisova & Vera Petrashevitch
2010	Tatsiana Uvarova & Callie Whitlock

Year	Mixed's Doubles Champions
1996	Carl Clark & Julie Kaczmarek
1997	Fredrik Eliasson & Martina Nedelkova
1998	Carl Clark & Julie Kaczmarek
1999	Carl Clark & Julie Kaczmarek
2000	Ryan Davidson & Julie Shiflet
2001	Trevor Spracklin & Jessica Arthur
2002	Hugo Alomar & Barbara Zahnova
2003	Ben Schreiber & Julie Kaczmarek
2004	Carl Clark & Julie Kaczmarek
2005	Zoltan Csanadi & Nataly Fleishman

Mid-Atlantic Clay Court Championships

By Tom Hood

In 1999, the Virginia State Clay Court Championships moved from Briarwood to Salisbury Country Club. Scott Steinour was the tournament director, and Bill Barnes and his McDonald's restaurants were the title sponsors. That first year there were a total of ten sponsors, prize money totaling $12,000 and 120 entries. Things were cruising along when, in true Texas fashion, thoughts turned bigger.

"The tournament had evolved and was to move on to something bigger, something that would include players from outside the Richmond area," said Barnes.

In 2006, Barnes and Steinour decided to switch from a state tournament to the USTA/Mid-Atlantic Section Clay Court Championships. Bullseye! This change had a tremendous effect on the tournament because entries were not restricted and could come from anywhere in the world. Drawing from a larger pool, the overall quality of play soared and so did the fan interest. People came to watch local heroes compete with former world-ranked players. The tournament soon became a gathering place where tennis players could meet up with old playing buddies and reminisce or sit back and watch the awesome talent displayed on the courts. Each year the level of play increased, so did the fun, and so did the fans. The success led to so many people coming out to watch that it almost seemed to be a party with a tournament instead of a tournament with a party.

Each year consideration is given to what can be done to enhance the tournament. In 2010, a permanent skybox was added allowing for a full view of all the courts and making the tournament one of the premier tennis events in the region. Open to all levels, this tournament offers the opportunity for the club player to match his or her skills with former and future stars. The event was recognized for its success in 2009 when it received USTA/Mid-Atlantic Section Tournament of the Year award. The skyward trend continued in 2011 with prize money of $30,000, 60 sponsors and 270 entries, and there is no sign of it slowing down!

USTA/Virginia Clay Court Championships (1999-2005)

USTA/Mid-Atlantic Clay Court Championships (2006-present)

at Salisbury Country Club

	MEN'S SINGLES	MENS DOUBLES	WOMEN"S SINGLES	WOMENS DOUBLES	MIXED
1999	Carl Clark def. Sean Steinour 6-3, 6-1	Carl Clark/Kurt Hammerschmidt def. Sean Steinour/Scott Steinour 6-4, 7-5	Tari Ann Toro def. Rachel Gale 6-4, 6-2	Rachel Gale/Julie Kaczmerck def. Tari Ann Toro/Williams 7-5, 6-0	Scott Steinour/Tari Ann Toro def. Joe Cappellino/Rachel Gale 7-5, 7-5
2000	John Winter def. Sean Steinour 6-3, 7-6	Sean Steinour/Scott Steinour def. Carl Clark/Kurt Hammerschmidt 7-5, 6-1	Kristin Lanio def. Rachel Gale 2-6, 6-3, 6-3	Rachel Gale/Julie Kaczmarek def. (finalist and score not available)	Carl Clark/Julie Kaczmarek def. Joe Cappellino/Rachel Gale 5-7, 6-4, 6-2
2001	Carl Clark def. Jay Bruner 7-6, 6-1	Carl Clark/Cris Robinson def. Sean Steinour/Scott Steinour 7-5, 1-6, 6-0	Kristin Elim def. Rachel Gale 7-6, 6-2	Bridget Bruner/Rachel Gale def. Margie Walsh/Tami Bigger 4-6, 6-3, 7-5	Joe Cappellino/Rachel Gale def. Jamie Hevron/Margie Walsh 6-3, 7-5
2002	Trevor Spracklin def. Carl Clark 7-6, 4-6, 6-1	Carl Clark/Trevor Spracklin def. Sean Steinour/Scott Steinour 6-4, 6-4	Melissa Robinson def. Lindsey Wyeth 6-1, 6-2	Rachel Gale/Julie Kaczmarek def. Margie Walsh/Tami Bigger 6-0, 6-0	Joe Cappellino/Rachel Gale def. Jay Bruner/Lindsey Howard score not available
2003	Daniel Casquero def. Carl Clark 5-7, 6-2, 6-3	Steinour/ Steinour def. Carl Clark/Trevor Spracklin 0-6, 6-3, 6-4	Lindsey Wyeth def. Chrissie Seredni 6-4, 6-2	Rachel Gale/Julie Kaczmarek def. Amy Mitchell/Kimberly Nantz 6-2, 6-1	Sean Steinour/Margie Walsh def. Joe Cappellino/ Rachel Gale 6-3, 5-7, 6-4
2004	Daniel Casquero def. Trevor Spracklin 4-6, 7-6, 7-5	Carl Clark/Trevor Spracklin def. Sean Steinour/Scott Steinour 6-1, 6-1	Bridget Merrick def. Chrissie Seredni 6-7, 6-3, 6-3	Julie Kaczmarek/ Bridget Merrick def. Rachel Gale/Lindsey Wyeth 6-3, 3-6, 6-1	Bridget Merrick/ Trevor Spracklin def. Sean Steinour/Margie Walsh 6-3, 7-6
2005	Matt Scott def. Trevor Spracklin 6-3, 6-4	Matt Scott/Trevor Spracklin def. def. Sean Steinour/Scott Steinour 6-2,6-4	Nataly Fleishman def. Lindsey Howard 6-1,6-0	Rachel Gale/Julie Kaczmarek def. Lindsey Howard/ Kate Harrington 6-1,6-3	Julie Kaczmarek/Matt Scott def. Sean Steinour/Margie Walsh 7-6, 7-5
2006	Evghenii Corduneanu def. Trevor Spracklin 4-6,6-3,6-2	Carl Clark/Trevor Spracklin def. Treat Huey/Andrew Downing 7-6, 6-4	Blakeley Griffith def. Alison Ojeda 6-4, 6-3	Alison Ojeda/Melissa Schaub def. Rachel Gale/Julie Kaczmarek 6-2,6-4	Alison Ojeda/David McNamara def. Trevor Spracklin/ Tami Bigger 6-3,6-3
2007	Oren Montevassel def. David McNamara 4-6, 7-5, 6-2	David McNamara/Oren Montevassel def. Iriarte/Lynch 6-3, 6-4	Petra Rampre def. Nataly Fleishman 6-0, 6-4	Nataly Fleishman/Petra Rampre def. Alison Ojeda/Melissa Schaub 6-0, 6-3	Oren Montevassel/Petra Rampre def. David McNamara/Alison Ojeda 6-3, 7-5
2008	Treat Huey def. David McNamara 7-6, 6-7, 7-5	David McNamara/Andreas Siljestroem def. Carl Clark/Trevor Spracklin 3-6, 6-1, 7-6	Petra Rampre def. Shadisha Robinson 6-3, 6-1	Caitlin Collins/Shadisha Robinson def. Alison Ojeda/Melissa Schaub 4-6, 7-5, 6-2	Salifu Mohammed/Petra Rampre def. Romain Ambert/Olga Borisova 6-4, 4-6, 6-2
2009	Drew Courtney def. David McNamara 6-1, 6-2	Milo Johnson/Sanam Singh def. Trevor Spracklin/Huntley Montgomery 7-6 (7-4), 6-2	Petra Rampre def. Tatsiana Uvarova 6-0, 3-0 ret	Petra Rampre/Chrissie Seredni def. Alison Ojeda/Melissa Schaub 6-4, 3-6, 7-6	Petra Rampre/Salifu Mohammed def. Katarina Yergina/Martin Stiegwardt 6-1, 6-2
2010	Michal Ciszek def. Sanam Singh 6-4, 7-6	Sergio Rojas/Sanam Singh def. Damon Martin/Tony Mule 6-1, 6-2	Petra Rampre def. Anna Mamalat 6-4, 6-1	Olga Borisova/Petra Rampre def. Emily Fraser/Amanda Rales 6-2, 6-3	David McNamara/Natasha Marks def. Romain Ambert/Petra Rampre 6-3, 6-4
2011	Jarmere Jenkins def. John Peers 6-4, 6-2	Michal Ciszek/Carl Clark def. Romain Ambert/ Martin Stiegwardt 7-6, 3-6, 6-3	Lenka Broosova def. Tatsiana Uvarova 6-1, 6-1	Lenka Broosova/Li Xi def. Lena Leonchuk/ Kateryna Yergina 3-6, 6-4, 7-5	Lenka Broosova/John Peers def. Carl Clark/Li Xi 6-4, 6-2

2011 women's singles champion Lenka Broosova gives her post-victory speech while tournament director Scott Steinour looks on.

2010 McDonald's Mid-Atlantic Clay Court men's singles champion Michal Ciszek.

"World's Largest Tennis Tournament"

By John Packett

Hugh Waters, III was always looking for something out of the ordinary to do when he was teaching tennis in Richmond.

And the long-time area pro may have come up with one of his most intriguing ideas during the summer of 1983.

Waters decided to put together what he referred to as the World's Largest Tennis Tournament, with an eye toward getting enough players in the field so that he could present the total to the Guinness Book of World Records.

"I've always kind of liked records," said Waters. "It just seemed like a good thing to get people playing tennis and do something neat."

Waters said the intention was to have a draw of 10,000 but the final total was 2,032. That's still a pretty healthy field.

Michelob Light was the sponsor, with a trip for two to Hilton Head Island, S.C., going to the winner. All of the participants were eligible for a drawing for the grand prize of a trip for two for a week in Barbados in the Caribbean.

The final was held at the old Arena (next to what was then Parker Field), and Tony Velo beat Leonard Booker for the top prize.

The tournament was open to everyone — male and female — and the entry fee was $10.

"The concept was you just played [a best-of-three sets match]," Waters said. "It didn't matter whether you were a girl or a boy, a kid or an adult, you just played. Nobody was seeded and there were no divisions. When we got to the final 16, it was pretty competitive."

Hugh Waters came up with the idea for the World's Largest Tennis Tournament.

Velo, who played for the University of Richmond and attended dental school at the Medical College of Virginia, defeated Hugh Waters, IV at Byrd Park in the semis before meeting Booker.

"All I can remember is Hoofy [Hugh Waters, IV) was starting to play very well," said Velo, who makes his home in Sun Valley, Idaho. "His game was coming around. There was a time when the Hoof got really good. I mean, I was in dental school at the time.

"Lenny was a guy who could run down everything," said Velo, who relied on his big serve.

"He could keep me out there for a long time. I just remember that it was super hot at the Arena during the summer, and I was lucky to win the match."

Velo, who won the Middle Atlantic Lawn Tennis Association men's singles title in 1979 and was runner-up in the state tournament that year, said he never got to take the trip to Hilton Head because of work at dental school.

"Winning [World's Largest Tournament] was nice, but I'd say the Middle Atlantic was my best win," said Velo.

When it was over, Waters contacted the Guinness Book of World Records but they refused to recognize it.

"They said they didn't have a category for it," said Waters. "I've been tempted to submit it again sometime."

Maybe it wasn't officially recognized as the World's Largest Tennis Tournament by the Guinness Book of World Records, but it's hard to imagine any other city putting together a tournament with 2,000 or more players in it.

Tony Velo (left), winner, and Leonard Booker (right), finalist, of World's Largest Tennis Tournament.

The Match They Thought Would Never End

By John Packett

Richmond is no longer home to either of the professional tours. However, the city can claim a couple of women's records that likely will never be broken.

Both of them occurred in a Ginny of Richmond match on Sept. 24, 1984 at Raintree Swim and Racquet Club between Vicki Nelson Dunbar and Jean Hepner, a pair of tenacious baseline players who kept the ball in play seemingly forever.

In fact, they kept trading ground strokes long enough to produce a rally that has gone down in history as the longest recorded point ever played in a pro tennis match. It lasted 643 shots and took 29 minutes before Nelson Dunbar ended it with a winner.

"I thought I was going to go crazy," Nelson Dunbar said after the match, which was celebrated in an article in the New York Times that was published on the 25th anniversary of the match in 2009.

"No matter what I did with the ball, she kept getting it back. We were both pretty much standing on the baseline lobbing. It took me a long time to get up the nerve to come in, but she finally hit a short lob and I put [the ball] away forever."

Nelson Dunbar's 6-4, 7-6 (13-11) victory is also the longest match in women's pro history at six hours and 31 minutes. The tiebreaker alone took one hour and 47 minutes, with the 643-stroke point coming at 11-10 (set point for Hepner).

Had Hepner won that point, the match would have gone to a third set and would have had to be completed the next day. As it was, the match didn't end until nearly midnight, when the two exhausted players finally left the court.

"I was surprised at how much time had elapsed," said Hepner. "That's what happens when you are under the alpha state of concentration!"

The match remained the longest in history for men or women, until Fabrice Santoro outlasted Arnaud Clement 16-14 in the fifth set of a French Open, first-round match in 2004. That match lasted two minutes longer and went five sets on clay.

That record has since been surpassed by John Isner and Nicolas Mahut, who played 11 hours and five minutes over three days at Wimbledon in 2010 before Isner finally prevailed 70-68 in the fifth set of the first-rounder.

The women's match was on a hard court and was only two sets — of the most boring tennis imaginable.

Hugh Waters, III, who was the owner of Raintree at the time, didn't necessarily think it was bad tennis.

"It was amusing to me how one of them would attack the net," Waters said. "They'd lob her and the next thing you know, they were both at the baseline. Then, the other one would come to the net. They wouldn't put anything away. They'd push it back."

"It was pure guts. Nobody's fussing about that long match Isner played [at Wimbledon]. They think it's gutsy. These girls didn't take a chance. They were gutting it out. I admire that. I thought it was a pretty damn neat match."

How do we know all these facts and figures about the match? Because the author of this article was there, chronicling it for the Richmond Times-Dispatch. It just seemed like such an unusual match that counting the exchanges became necessary at some point.

And all these years later, I'm glad I kept track of it so the women's tour would recognize it. Thank goodness it didn't go three sets!

Jean Hepner

Vicki Nelson Dunbar

Charity Exhibitions

By Eric Perkins

Over the years, Richmond has hosted numerous high-profile exhibitions and special events featuring many of the world's greatest players, and in the process, raised over $1 million for charitable causes.

Undeterred from his crushing defeat at the hands of Billie Jean King in the legendary "Battle of the Sexes" match in the Houston Astrodome in 1973, Bobby Riggs entertained a crowd of over 2,000 at the Westwood Club in October 1974, playing a series of singles and doubles matches—all while wearing a ladies' tennis dress—against some of the area's top women players at the time, including Lindsay Burn Wortham, Lloyd Hatcher, Betty Baugh Harrison, and Flo Bryan.

In 1982, Best Products was one of the nation's premier catalog showroom retail chains, with its corporate headquarters on Parham Road. That summer, the company sponsored the Best Products Summer Challenge which saw Jimmy Connors defeat Bjorn Borg 6-4, 3-6, 7-5, 6-3 in a hard-fought match at a sold-out Richmond Coliseum. Net proceeds benefited the newly formed Richmond Tennis Foundation, a local nonprofit organized by Paddi Valentine to pursue a community indoor tennis center project.

In November 1985, John McEnroe's "Tennis Over America" exhibition tour came to town, with McEnroe winning a methodical 4-6, 6-1, 6-4 victory over Bjorn Borg before an estimated crowd of 8,000 people. The opening act featured Wade McGuire-Valerie Farmer defeating Keith Mumford-Leslie Seward 8-6.

Flash forward to the 1990s, John McEnroe beat Jimmy Connors 6-3, 7-5 in an exhibition match at the Robins Center on the University of Richmond campus before an estimated crowd of 9,200 on September 25, 1994. The Richmond Tennis Association helped organize the event. Top local talent Jamie Hevron and David Caldwell played a pro set match to kick off the festivities. The event raised over $100,000 to benefit the Richmond Cerebral Palsy Center.

Former world number one Jim Courier paid a special visit to Richmond in 2001 to play in an exhibition match against former ATP pro and Richmond Tennis Hall of Famer Wade McGuire to benefit Noah's Children, a local nonprofit organization that is now a program of Bon Secours Richmond that provides the only pediatric hospice and palliative care program in Central Virginia (and one of the first in the United States). McGuire and Courier also shared tips with local players at tennis clinics held at Willow Oaks Country Club as part of the festivities. While the main event featured a singles victory for Courier over his friend McGuire, the record will reflect that local pros Carl Clark and Sean Steinour defeated the Courier-McGuire team 6-4 in a special exhibition set to conclude a fun evening of tennis. Another exhibition match saw Courier and McGuire pair up with local tennis supporters Neil Gulati and Dr. Rakesh Jain. They were the top bidders in a silent auction for the opportunity to play

Jim Courier and Wade McGuire played during a charity exhibition in 2001 to benefit Noah's Children at the Westwood Club..

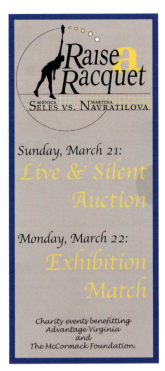

with the pros and enjoyed a memorable tennis experience while supporting a great cause.

March 2004 marked the first of a series of exhibition matches held at VCU's Siegel Center with all-time great Martina Navratilova beating another former world No. 1 and International Tennis Hall of Famer Monica Seles 6-4, 7-6. In an opening mixed doubles match, Seles and Carl Clark edged Navratilova and Sean Steinour 8-5. Net proceeds from the event and a silent auction benefited the McCormack Foundation and a local community initiative known as Advantage Richmond, which was organized to help position Richmond as a world-class tennis destination.

In September 2004, Serena Williams defeated Jennifer Capriati 7-6, 2-6, 6-3 in front of a sellout crowd of 6,600 at the Siegel Center. This was a charity event sponsored by Anthem that raised over $350,000 for the VCU Massey Cancer Center.

Andre Agassi interacting with kids during an October 2006 visit to the Mary and Frances Youth Center at VCU. The junior clinic, featuring Agassi and his wife Stefanie Graf, was organized by Lobs & Lessons as part of the Genworth Children's Advantage Classic festivities that year.

In the opening match, Meghan Shaughnessy beat Alexandra Stevenson in a pro set. As in other charity exhibitions, the players participated in various junior clinics and other activities leading up to the match, including a special "Q and A" luncheon at the Westwood Club. The main event was a much-anticipated rematch of the 2004 U.S. Open quarterfinal where Capriati prevailed 2-6, 6-4, 6-4 in a hard-fought match that saw one of the worst officiating calls in U.S. Open history go against Williams and, arguably, play a role in the outcome of the match.

The following year witnessed the debut of the Genworth Children's Advantage Classic at the Siegel Center, which featured another match-up of former world number ones—Andre Agassi, Stefanie Graf and Andy Roddick. A sellout crowd of 6,000 saw the husband and wife team of Agassi-Graf narrowly defeat Roddick-Anna Kournikova 8-7. In the men's singles main event, Agassi defeated Roddick 7-6, 6-4 in an entertaining match. The event raised over $500,000 to support two local nonprofit organizations--Lobs & Lessons and the William Byrd Community House.

The Genworth Children's Advantage Classic returned to the Siegel Center in 2006 with another all-star lineup featuring Andre Agassi, world top ten player James Blake, Stefanie Graf, and former world No. 1 and three-time Grand Slam singles champion Lindsay Davenport. A group of local charities shared the net proceeds from the event, estimated at over $500,000. The charities, all of which serve at-risk youth in the Richmond community, included Big Brothers Big Sisters, Boys & Girls Club, Comfort Zone Camp, FRIENDS Association for Children, Stop Child Abuse Now, William Byrd Community House, and YMCA.

Agassi and Graf returned to Richmond in October 2007 to participate in the Genworth Children's Advantage Classic, but rather than play an exhibition match, the two tennis legends participated in a youth tennis clinic at the Mary and Frances Youth Center and hosted a youth fair that featured fun and educational activities promoting healthy living. A concert by James Taylor at the Siegel Center highlighted the festivities.

Jennifer Capriati

On September 12, 2008, the Anthem Live! event at the Siegel Center featured Roddick defeating Blake 6-4, 6-3 before a crowd of over 4,500. Mike Bryan and Roddick teamed up to beat Blake and John Isner (a last-minute sub for an injured Bob Bryan) 8-3 in the opener. The event raised an estimated $350,000 to fund cancer research. The Anthem Live! series was particularly special to James Blake, who dedicated his efforts to the memory of his father, Thomas, who died of cancer in 2004.

Women's Pro Tour Comes to Richmond

By John Packett

The women's professional tennis circuit has indeed come a long way, baby, since its early days, but the high-powered tour got a huge boost during its infancy from Dorothy Chewning and the Westwood Racquet Club.

In 1970, when there wasn't a separate women's circuit and the U.S. Tennis Association wanted to keep the girls from forming their own tour, Philip Morris and Westwood came to the rescue by letting them have a venue to stage a tournament.

And Chewning, who had been responsible for some ladies invitationals at Westwood in the late 1960s, made sure it happened.

"She was the instigator," said Betty Gustafson, who worked with Chewning in the early years of the invitational and later what became the Virginia Slims International in helping secure some of the best players in the world.

"She worked hard and she got the players. I remember going with her to New York to talk to the players about coming here. We had the best in the world at the time. Margaret Court, Billie Jean King, Rosie Casals, Peaches Bartkowicz, Maria Bueno.

"She wasn't very athletic, but she loved the game. She loved to watch it. She was a real businesswoman, too."

Martina Navratilova won back-to-back Central Fidelity titles in 1979-80 as she ascended to a world No. 1 ranking. *Courtesy of Richmond Times-Dispatch.*

Houston held the first Virginia Slims tournament but the second one, in November 1970, was staged at Westwood, thanks to Chewning, who was good friends with Gladys Heldman, the creator of the first women's pro circuit.

King defeated Nancy Richey 6-3, 6-3 in the singles final and claimed the doubles title with Casals.

"The tennis was marvelous," said Gustafson, who was among an SRO crowd who watched the two long-time rivals slug it out.

The circuit skipped Richmond in 1971, but returned in 1972 and '73. King beat Richey again in the '72 title match, and didn't return to defend the following year. That's when Court dominated the field, whipping Janet Newberry in the final.

Billie Jean King addresses the crowd at Westwood after winning her first title on the new Virginia Slims Tour in 1970. *Courtesy of Richmond Times-Dispatch.*

Former men's Wimbledon champion Bobby Riggs attended the 1973 tournament to scout Court for an upcoming Battle of the Sexes match. Evidently, Riggs picked up quite a few pointers because he defeated Court easily later that year.

"I thought it would be a good idea to watch her play," said Riggs, who was 55 at the time. "I'll see if I can find some flaws or a weakness in her game. Something that would give me an idea of how to play her. I'd hate to let the men in the country down by losing."

Tracy Austin was runner-up in the 1982 tournament. *Courtesy of Richmond Times-Dispatch.*

With larger cities and bigger purses vying for a spot on the circuit, Chewning and Richmond were unable to keep the event at Westwood. That was unfortunate and especially disappointing to Chewning, who had helped get the tour off the ground.

The women's circuit returned in 1979 as the Central Fidelity Banks International to begin a five-year run at the Robins Center.

Martina Navratilova, the world's No. 1 player, captured the first two Central Fidelity events. The draw for the first one contained 17 of the world's top 20 players, but the tournament wasn't able to attract that kind of field again.

Tracy Austin, Wendy Turnbull and Virginia Wade were among the headliners. However, the fact that the tournament was held indoors in the summer made it difficult to get both players and fans to show up, and it ceased to exist following the 1983 affair.

Even though it's been gone for nearly three decades, women's pro tennis remains a vivid memory for many Richmonders, who won't soon forget the contributions made to the sport by Chewning and her friends.

"She put her heart into it," said Gustafson. "She spent a lot of time getting it organized. She would find housing for the players. She found people to take them out to dinner. It was a very big part of her life for those years she was in it."

Virginia Slims of Richmond

1970   Billie Jean King def Nancy Richey 6-3, 6-3
1972   Billie Jean King def Nancy Richey 6-3, 6-4
1973   Margaret Court def Janet Newberry 6-2, 6-1

Central Fidelity Banks International

1979   Martina Navratilova def Kathy Jordan 6-1, 6-3
1980   Martina Navratilova def Mary Lou Piatek 6-3, 6-0
1981   Mary Lou Piatek def Sue Barker 6-4, 6-1
1982   Wendy Turnbull def Tracy Austin 6-7, 6-4, 6-2
1983   Ros Fairbank def Kathy Jordan 6-4, 5-7, 6-4

Richmond - Major Stop on the Men's Pro Tour

By John Packett

In the summer of 1965, flamboyant (to put it mildly) promoter Bill Riordan was looking for a tournament to fill out his Caribbean circuit.

Richmond is over 1,000 miles from the palm trees and warm breezes of the Caribbean islands, but that became the impetus for the Fidelity Bankers Life Invitational men's tennis tournament that started at The Arena in February of 1966.

Riordan contacted Lou Einwick, who was president of the Richmond Tennis Patrons Association, and asked about putting an event here.

"He came to me and said, 'Gee, wouldn't it be great if you ran a tournament in Richmond, Virginia?'" Einwick recalled.

Einwick thought it might be a good way to raise money for the RTPA, as well as bring big-time tournament tennis to Richmond. So he told Riordan OK.

Thus began a 19-year love affair between men's tennis and the city that played out at The Arena and later the Coliseum. Einwick served as tournament director of every one of the events, spending many hours every year dealing with players, fans and officials.

Most of the world's best players traded ground strokes and service returns for nearly two decades, providing many memorable matches and unforgettable scenes that were enjoyed by thousands of fans.

From hometown hero Arthur Ashe to Rod Laver to Ilie Nastase to Bjorn Borg to John McEnroe and Stefan Edberg, the tournament earned a reputation as one of the finest indoor events on the circuit – even though it was held in one of the smallest cities on the tour.

After lining up The Arena and a sponsor in Fidelity Bankers Life Insurance, all Einwick had to do was find some players. Those were the days when most of the top players were amateurs, and tournament prizes were motorcycles and color TVs.

The first player Einwick tried to get was Ashe, who had developed into one of world's top players despite growing up in segregated Richmond of the 1950s and 60s and not being allowed to play on most of the public courts.

(l to r) Terry Addison, Colin Dibley, Roy Emerson and Rod Laver await the start of the 1973 Doubles Final - UVB Classic. *Courtesy of Richmond Times-Dispatch.*

"One of the things that made the tournament a tremendous success at first was no one had ever seen Arthur Ashe play tennis in Richmond," said Einwick. "He was the new hot player on the USTA [United States Tennis Association] circuit at the time."

Einwick also enlisted another Richmonder, Bitsy Harrison, to entice local fans and added six other players to the eight-man field. The draw was filled out with Chuck McKinley, Gene Scott, Ian Crookenden, Cliff Richey, Frank Froehling and Charlie Pasarell.

Froehling spoiled Ashe's return when he beat the Richmond native in the first round but Ashe later won the tournament three times.

"One of the ironies that may have helped that first tournament was that in 1966 we had a tremendous snowstorm," said Einwick. "The schools had been closed all week and nobody could go anywhere. "

"That Thursday and Friday, the snow finally melted and people could get out. I think people just wanted to get out of the house."

Arthur Ashe with one of his three UVB trophies. *Courtesy of Richmond Times-Dispatch.*

One of the most memorable moments of the first tournament came when a linesman called a foot fault on Richey at set point at 19-20 in the opening set against Crookenden. The sometimes-violatile Richey maintained his composure and went on to win in three sets.

"I think it was the only foot fault called the whole time," said Einwick. "And it came on the second serve. I think the saving grace was Crookenden crushed the return and it was sort of a moot point. Richey just glared at the linesman but didn't say anything."

Another interesting event occurred during the final tournament at The Arena in 1971 when a soft-drink canister exploded under the stands and had some fans heading for the exits, not knowing exactly what was going on.

The unsettling noise from the dispenser came during the singles final between Ashe and Nastase, and it took a reassuring message from chair umpire John Pope that nothing serious had happened so the match could continue.

Einwick's other memory from the early days was using a canvas court spread over The Arena's floor, making the surface extremely fast.

"That first tournament, we were renting Riordan's court, but it was in Salisbury, Maryland, and we had had all that snow," Einwick said. "Mr. Ashe [Arthur's father] drove up there when nobody else was moving and brought it back. I don't know how he did it."

Ilie Nastase pleads his case.

Ashe won two of the six tournaments at The Arena and lost in the final twice, so he represented Richmond well during the early days of the Fidelity Invitational and helped make the tournament a rousing success as a top drawing card.

When the Coliseum opened in the fall of 1971, it presented Einwick the opportunity to move the event in 1972 to more spacious surroundings in a state-of-the-art facility. And so 12 of the last 13 editions of the tournament were held on Leigh Street. The 1983 event was held at the Robins Center.

By now, the Lamar Hunt-led World Championship Tennis organization was supplying players, so Einwick didn't have to worry about recruiting. He did, however, have to be concerned about whether they would always show up as promised.

The size of the fields grew to eventually 32 players, and for a while, two courts were placed side by side on the Coliseum floor, with a netting separating them. That caused some distractions for the players, and the format was changed back to one court in 1979.

United Virginia Bank took over sole sponsorship of the tournament in 1976 and remained in that position until the end.

There were some amazing matches over the years, including the great one between Borg and McEnroe, when Borg saved eight match points and pulled out a three-set victory over McEnroe in the 1979 semifinals.

The preceding year, the field had been considered the strongest in the world outside of the four Grand Slam tournaments. That was also the year that five linesmen walked off the court during the doubles final to protest being berated all week by Vitas Gerulaitis and others.

Frenchman Yannick Noah won his first pro tournament in 1981, beating Ivan Lendl, who had to retire in the second set because of an injury.

Einwick decided to give up his job as tournament director after the 1984 tournament, and UVB felt it was unable to put any more sponsorship dollars into the event following that year. When no other corporation stepped forward as a sponsor, the tournament left town.

When Borg was forced to default one year because of a stomach injury rather than use a painkiller to continue, one spectator commented that the Swede had used medication at Wimbledon to play. One of the players, Sherwood Stewart, replied, "Yeah, but this ain't Wimbledon."

It may not have been Wimbledon, but it was the closest most Richmonders would ever get to the best tennis in the world.

Results from the Fidelity Bankers Life/UVB Tennis Classic

Year	Singles Final
1966	Chuck McKinley d. Frank Froehling 6-1, 6-2
1967	Charles Pasarell d. Arthur Ashe 6-3, 8-6
1968	Arthur Ashe d. Chuck McKinley 6-2, 6-1
1969	Clark Graebner d. Tom Koch 6-3, 10-12, 9-7
1970	Arthur Ashe d. Stan Smith 6-2, 13-11
1971	Illie Nastase d. Arthur Ashe 3-6, 6-2, 6-4
1972	Rod Laver d. Cliff Drysdale 2-6, 6-3, 7-5, 6-3
1973	Rod Laver d. Roy Emerson 6-4, 6-3
1974	Illie Nastase d. Tom Gorman 6-2, 6-3
1975	Bjorn Borg d. Arthur Ashe 4-6, 6-4, 6-4
1976	Arthur Ashe d. Brian Gottfried 6-2, 6-4
1977	Tom Okker d. Vitas Gerulaitis 3-6, 6-3, 6-4
1978	Vitas Gerulaitis d. John Newcombe 6-3, 6-4
1979	Bjorn Borg d. Guillermo Vilas 6-3, 6-1
1980	John McEnroe d. Roscoe Tanner 6-1, 6-2
1981	Yannick Noah d. Ivan Lendl 6-1, 3-1, retired
1982	Jose-Luis Clerc d. Fritz Buehning 3-6, 6-3, 6-4, 6-3
1983	Guillermo Vilas d. Steve Denton 6-3, 7-5, 6-4
1984	John McEnroe d. Steve Denton 6-3, 7-6
	Doubles Final
1966	Chuck McKinley-Gene Scott d. Arthur Ashe-Cliff Richey 6-8, 8-6, 7-5
1967	Arthur Ashe-Charles Pasarell d. Cliff Drysdale-Ronald Holmberg 6-1, 6-4
1968	Arthur Ashe-Charles Pasarell d. Ronald Holmberg-Bob Lutz 6-4, 6-4
1969	Robert McKinley-Jim McManus d. Clark Graebner-Cliff Richey 7-5, 3-6, 7-5
1970	Arthur Ashe-Charles Pasarell d. Stan Smith-Jim McManus 9-7, 6-2
1971	Arthur Ashe-Dennis Ralston d. John Newcombe-Ken Rosewall 7-6, 3-6, 7-6
1972	Tom Okker-Marty Riessen d. John Newcombe-Tony Roche 7-6, 7-6
1973	Roy Emerson-Rod Laver d. Terry Addison-Colin Dibley 3-6, 6-3, 6-4
1974	Nikki Pilic-Allan Stone d. John Alexander-Phil Dent 6-3, 3-6, 7-6
1975	Hans Kary-Fred McNair d. Paolo Bertolucci-Adriano Panatta 7-6, 5-7, 7-6
1976	Brian Gottfried-Raul Ramirez d. Arthur Ashe-Tom Okker 6-4, 7-5
1977	Wojtek Fibak-Tom Okker d. Ross Case-Tony Roche 6-4, 6-4
1978	Bob Hewitt-Frew McMillan d. Vitas Gerulaitis-Sandy Mayer 6-3, 7-5
1979	Brian Gottfried-John McEnroe d. Ion Tiriac-Guillermo Vilas 6-4, 6-3
1980	Fritz Buehning-Johan Kriek d. Brian Gottfried-Frew McMillan 3-6, 6-3, 7-6
1981	Tim Gullickson-Bernard Mitton d. Brian Gottfried-Raul Ramirez 3-6, 6-2, 6-3
1982	Mark Edmondson-Kim Warwick d. Syd Ball-Rolf Gehring 6-4, 6-2
1983	Pavel Slozil-Tomas Smid d. Fritz Buehning-Brian Teacher 6-2, 6-4
1984	John McEnroe-Patrick McEnroe d. Kevin Curren-Steve Denton 7-6, 6-2

Revenge of the Linesmen

By John Packett

It's rare for a doubles match to upstage the singles final but that's exactly what happened on the last day of the 1978 United Virginia Bank Tennis Classic at the Coliseum.

In what was likely the most unusual – and ugliest – occurrence during any of the men's tournaments in Richmond, five linesmen walked off the court during the doubles to protest the atrocious treatment of officials by the players, in particular Vitas Gerulaitis.

One of them, Dick Blanton, turned and gave Gerulaitis the finger, the same obscene gesture the American had resorted to against the volunteer officials on several occasions during the week-long tournament.

While this incident may have been the worst, it was far from the only one that took place during the annual men's visit to Richmond. A number of other players verbally abused the officials throughout the affair, but none were as bad as Gerulaitis.

"Right from the get-go in 1978, we were having difficulties we hadn't had before," said tournament director Lou Einwick, who pointed out that two courts were still being used and it caused distractions. "My observation was everybody came from Philadelphia [site of U.S. Pro Indoor] upset, and that upsetness continued on here."

Dick Blanton walks off the court in protest.
Courtesy of Richmond Times-Dispatch.

Prior to the doubles final, Gerulaitis had been involved in another incident, where he severely criticized the tournament referee for what he perceived as indecisiveness for not removing a chair umpire who was calling foot faults on him.

Gerulaitis was not defaulted – as he could have been for his verbal abuse of officials – and he went on to win the singles final over John Newcombe. After the final, Gerulaitis gave a conciliatory speech and complimented the tournament.

The compliments did not last long. A few minutes later, Gerulaitis and Sandy Mayer began their doubles final against the top-seeded team of Bob Hewitt and Frew McMillan, generally regarded as one of the best teams of all-time.

In the third game of the opening set, Hewitt fell behind love-40 on his serve and Gerulaitis hit what appeared to be a winner just inside the baseline. The base linesman, John Rose, called it out, however, and wouldn't yield to chair umpire Sue Cain, who thought it was in.

Instead of the game being over in favor of Gerulaitis and Mayer, play continued, and Hewitt

Dick Blanton makes a gesture toward Vitas Gerulaitis. *Courtesy of Richmond Times-Dispatch.*

and McMillan won, taking a 2-1 lead. On the next-to-last point of that game, Gerulaitis slammed a ball that almost hit Rose, who stood up and pointed at Gerulaitis.

During the changeover, Mayer asked for and got the removal of Rose. When Rose was replaced, that's when five others walked off the court in protest. As he was leaving, Blanton turned and held up his middle finger. His gesture appeared in a newspaper photo the next day.

"I believe human dignity is far more important than any tennis match," Blanton said afterward. "When they replaced [Rose], that was it. My protest was for Gerulaitis' treatment of the linesman."

After a 10-minute delay, new linesmen replaced the ones who left and the match resumed. There were no further incidents, and Hewitt and McMillan won 6-3, 7-5. Because of all the problems in 1978, paid professional chair umpires were used for the remaining events here.

Gerulaitis didn't return to Richmond until 1984, when he and John McEnroe staged a competitive three-set semifinal before McEnroe went on to win the final UVB tournament.

Gerulaitis died of carbon monoxide poisoning in 1994 at age 40, when a propane heater malfunctioned when he was visiting a friend's home on Long Island. But his antics here will never be forgotten.

A Match to Remember

By John Packett

During its 19-year run, the men's indoor tennis tournament in Richmond produced some outstanding matches. There is no doubt, however, which one should be considered the best of the best ever played here.

It came in the semifinals of the 1979 United Virginia Bank Classic and electrified a Saturday night sellout crowd at the Coliseum.

Bjorn Borg and John McEnroe staged one of the most dramatic meetings of their fierce rivalry, when the Swede saved an incredible eight match points before finally subduing McEnroe in 2 1/2 hours 4-6, 7-6 (10-8), 6-3.

"It was not only a tremendously well-played match," said tournament director Lou Einwick, who didn't miss many matchups over the years. "Of course, you also had Borg wiggling out of all those match points."

McEnroe, who was 19 at the time, appeared to be cruising to a straight-sets victory over Borg. This was only the second meeting between the two young stars, with the New Yorker claiming the first one in Stockholm late in 1978.

Twice McEnroe had match point on Borg's serve in the 12th game of the second set, but the Swede erased both of them.

Then came the amazing tiebreaker. Borg took the first point only to have McEnroe reel off six of the next seven to assume a seemingly safe 6-2 advantage. That meant McEnroe had four match points. Win any one of them and it was over.

John McEnroe makes a return to Bjorn Borg.

But Borg proceeded to unleash four consecutive winners and scrambled back to 6-all.

"One of the things I recall is McEnroe serving on the other side [of the court] from where I'm sitting on one of the match points, and he hits a wicked, left-hand wide serve," said Einwick. "Ron Cain is on the [sideline] and he calls, 'Out.'

"The ball just missed but it did miss. I can't forget McEnroe glaring at [Cain]. Of everything in that match, that still sticks in my memory. If it had been an ace, the match was over with. It was a great serve but it just missed."

McEnroe had two more match points at 7-6 and 8-7 but back-to-back mistakes gave Borg life, and he capitalized. The stoic one stuck a forehand volley into an open court after a furious exchange at the net, then watched as McEnroe sent a service return wide.

"That match had everything," said Borg afterward. "A lot of good things. I was very lucky."

The final set was close through the first six games, before Borg took the final three to close it out.

Einwick recalled going into the locker room following the match and seeing an inconsolable McEnroe.

"He was sitting there with his head down," said Einwick. "I said something like 'Tough match,' and he never said a word. He just looked totally defeated in the thing."

Borg had enough left in the tank the next day to roll past Guillermo Vilas 6-3, 6-1 in a long, but lackluster, final. But the fans had more than gotten their money's worth the previous evening in watching two of the game's all-time best slug it out in a classic duel.

Bjorn Borg addresses the crowd at the Richmond Coliseum after winning the United Virginia Bank Classic in 1979. *Courtesy of Richmond Times-Dispatch.*

Seniors Tour

By Eric Perkins

Throughout the Open Era, a variety of different senior tours have served to extend the competitive careers of top players while providing audiences with high-quality tennis in a more entertaining, intimate atmosphere. Over the years, Richmond has been a popular stop on the senior circuits.

In the early 1970s, Richmond hosted two Grand Masters senior tour events at Briarwood in 1973 and Westwood in 1974. Denmark's Torben Ulrich (father of Lars Ulrich, who played competitive tennis as a junior in the early 80s but achieved worldwide fame as the drummer for heavy metal rock group Metallica) won both events, each time defeating Frank Sedgman in the final

When Jimmy Connors and Northern Virginia entrepreneur Ray Benton started their own senior tour in the mid 1990s, it did not take long for Richmond tennis community and business leaders—namely Trigon as a title sponsor—to step up and bring the Nuveen/Success Magazine Senior Tour to Richmond for a successful run from 1997-2001.

The 1997 event was held in late April at Robious Sport and Fitness Club in Midlothian (now known as Midlothian Athletic Club), and featured Jimmy Connors and Andres Gomez as the top seeds with a solid supporting cast of Yannick Noah—upset on opening night by Gene Mayer—Eddie Dibbs, Roscoe Tanner, Peter Fleming, Mel Purcell, John Lloyd, and crowd-favorite Mansour Bahrami. With a seating capacity of 3,000 in a stadium court erected specifically for the tournament, nearly 18,000 tennis fans enjoyed the inaugural Trigon Champions event despite unseasonably chilly and rainy weather that delayed or rained out several sessions, including the final, when Connors defeated Gomez 4-6, 6-3, 12-10 before a small crowd on a Tuesday morning.

In 1998, the event moved to a new home across the river at Hermitage Country Club. Despite a slightly smaller venue, the Hermitage events were nonetheless successful with roughly 15,000 in attendance and an even stronger field featuring Connors, Gomez, Guillermo Vilas, John McEnroe and Bjorn Borg, who made one brief appearance at the 1998 event, retiring after losing the first set of his opening match against Mansour Bahrami. The Hermitage events in particular featured a wide variety of special clinics, corporate hospitality, and a lot of golf. It's fair to say the players spent as much time on the golf course as the tennis court.

Connors continued his winning ways in Richmond by again capturing the title in 1998 (over Bahrami) and 1999 (over McEnroe). His luck ran out in 2000, however,

John McEnroe serves to Jimmy Connors in the 1999 Trigon Champions Final at Hermitage Country Club. Connors won the match in straight sets to earn his third consecutive title in Richmond.

when he lost round-robin matches to both Mats Wilander and Gomez, who advanced to the final but was soundly beaten by McEnroe 6-2, 6-3.

The festivities weren't limited to singles, and one entertaining aspect of the doubles events were the special appearances by local legends Tom Cain (who played in two of the events, partnering once with McEnroe and once with Carl Clark), Junie Chatman, Damian Sancilio, and Jon Ramthun.

The 2001 tournament was special in several ways. First, the event was moved indoors to the larger-capacity VCU Siegel Center in late September. Second, three-time champion Connors had curtailed his playing schedule by this point and was not in the draw. Sadly, the tragic events of September 11, 2001 cast an ominous shadow over the event (and the senior tour as a whole, which by the end of the year had drastically reduced its schedule and folded not long thereafter). McEnroe won the final edition of the VCU/Trigon Champions in Richmond by beating Wilander in straight sets.

John McEnroe, Tom Cain and Carl Clark pose after a practice session during the 2001 VCU/Trigon Seniors event.

Mats Wilander (above) and Jimmy Connors (right) competed in several of the Trigon Seniors events in Richmond.

USTA Pro Circuit Events

By Tom Hood

Dreams. Perhaps as a young girl at the age of eight you saw your mother win the club championship or as a young boy you watched the Wimbledon final with your dad. Whatever the reason, the initial seeds of the dream to play big-time tennis were planted. After years of practice and countless tournaments, it was time to give the big time a shot. But how do you get there? Unlike many other sports, tennis offers a way. It is called the satellite circuit. The satellite circuit is a proving ground for aspiring tennis players. It is a series of tournaments that offers modest prize money and ranking points. At the end of the series, ranking points are given to those with the best results and those players move on to bigger tournaments. Even though the satellites are considered the minor leagues of tennis, some great tennis is being played. One never knows when one may be witnessing an Andre Agassi clawing his way to the top.

In 1984, a $50,000 women's satellite tournament made a stop in Richmond at Raintree Swim and Racquet Club. The tournament, called "The Ginny of Richmond," was filled with talented players hoping for the big time. There was one regular tour player in the field, Joanne Russell, who handily won the event. Other players picked up valuable ranking points and experience, some of whom made it on the main women's tour. The Ginny of Richmond is remembered for something else as well. It was where the longest women's professional match in tennis history and the longest point were played, featured in more detail earlier in this book.

In 1981, the Penn satellite circuit made its first of five stops at Brandermill Country Club. The tournament was called the Investors Tennis Classic and consisted of a qualifying draw of 64 players battling for 16 places in the main draw. That first year local stars Mark Vines, Junie Chatman, Mark Buckley, Jim Milley, Tom Hood, John DePew, Norm Schellenger, Jr. and host pro Dave Snidow were offered the chance to compete with some of the best young talent on the circuit. Over the years other local players in the Investors Tennis Classic included Greg Miller, George Foreman and Drew Robinson. Future tour players Van Winitsky, Mel Purcell and Jimmy Arias all fulfilled their dreams in professional tennis after starting out on the Penn satellite circuit.

Ralph Whitaker Memorial

By Tom Hood

Let's just call January the beginning of "cabin fever" season. So the good folks at the Westwood Club put together a men's doubles tournament in honor of their foremost member, Ralph Whitaker, and named it the Ralph Whitaker Men's Invitational Tennis Tournament. The inaugural event was held January 1968. The draws for the tournament typically included the doubles teams from regional universities as well as some of the top local talent, but the occasional tour player (Charlie Owens) would make an appearance. Bob and Martha Perkins ran the tournament for years, putting on one of the most looked-forward-to events in the city. In 1994, after Ralph's death, the word "memorial" was incorporated into the title. The "Whitaker" went through some changes over the years, moving to the summer and becoming a singles tournament, but in 2000 the doubles matches returned. Today, the Westwood men's member-guest tournament bears Whitaker's name, continuing his legacy.

From left: Finalists of the first Ralph Whitaker Invitational Tournament at Westwood in January 1968 - Lee Fentress, Fred McNair, III, Dick Makepeace and Eddie Phillips. Fentress and McNair took the doubles title. *Courtesy of Richmond Times-Dispatch.*

Southeastern Open

By John Packett

Dr. John Watson.

Dr. John Watson loved to have a good time, and he always enjoyed himself immensely during the Southeastern Open.

With a smile on his face, Watson directed the long-running tournament at Brook Field and Battery Park for more than 40 years, until his failing health forced him to turn over the duties to Wayne Motley and Guy Walton before he passed away.

In its heyday, the Southeastern Open attracted players from as far away as New York City and Atlanta and was considered one of the top tournaments for African Americans in the days before blacks and whites were able to share the same courts.

"When social values changed, the tournament changed," said Bill Redd, referring to white folks eventually joining the festivities.

"It was always on Father's Day weekend," added Redd, who helped Watson with the tournament in the early days, when the Richmond Racquet Club was responsible for getting players and setting up the draws.

There would be a junior tournament on Friday, followed by adults in open and age-group divisions on Saturday and Sunday. Play would be continuous – as the entry form declared – meaning there wouldn't be much time between matches.

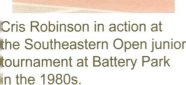

Cris Robinson in action at the Southeastern Open junior tournament at Battery Park in the 1980s.

"John always used two balls, instead of three [for the matches]," said John Royster, a long-time local referee who played in it on several occasions. The tournament also used no-ad scoring in an effort to speed up matches and free up courts.

"I know he used courts at John Marshall High School, Byrd Park and Battery Park," said Royster. "You would play a match and then 30 or 40 minutes later, you would play another one. I remember one time I played three matches in one day when I got to the final."

Many of the same players would show up year after year, Redd recalled, and made it seem almost like a family gathering.

Watson, who was the long-time coach at Virginia Union University, made sure everyone was well-fed, too, with hot dogs and hamburgers on the grill and watermelon for dessert in the shade of the trees surrounding the Battery Park courts.

"He had a big tournament over there for a long time," said Royster. "It was really well-attended."

In recent years, the draws have gotten smaller and smaller, but Motley and Walton have attempted to keep the event alive.

"The tournament ran its course," said Redd. "I used to look forward to the Southeastern."

Davis Cup

By Eric Perkins

The Davis Cup is one of the world's oldest and most prestigious international tennis competitions. Dwight F. Davis, a 21-year old Harvard graduate, first developed the concept in 1900 with several other members of the Harvard tennis team as an annual competition to promote international goodwill and friendship. Davis designed a format for the competition and commissioned a specially designed trophy that later would bear his name.

Initially the Davis Cup competition was limited to the United States and Great Britain, but gradually expanded and, in 2011, over 140 countries participated. The competition is now governed by the International Tennis Federation.

The United States has won the Davis Cup over 30 times and it should come as no surprise that Richmond has hosted a U.S. Davis Cup match, or "tie" (elimination round matches between teams are referred to as "ties," while individual matches are referred to as "rubbers"). Richmond was chosen to host a May 1968 tie pitting the U.S. squad against the British Caribbean team from the West Indies.

Proclaimed by Governor Godwin, who was the 60th and 62nd Governor of Virginia for two non-consecutive terms, as "the most significant tennis event in Virginia's history," the first round zonal match was held at Byrd Park. With just a few weeks' advance notice, the Richmond Tennis Association and its volunteer base worked closely with USTA and city officials to prepare the site and coordinate the hundreds of logistical details to ensure the success of the event. Individual-session tickets were sold at Byrd Park, Thalhimers, and Miller & Rhoads for $5.00 each.

Arthur Ashe led the U. S. team to victory in the 1968 Davis Cup competition. *Courtesy of Richmond Times-Dispatch.*

This event was particularly meaningful for Arthur Ashe, Sr., who recalled his son being heartbroken as a child after being turned away from the Byrd Park courts because of the city's segregated policy at that time and now triumphantly returning to those same courts to lead the U.S. team to victory. The event was also special for a young Tommy Cain and other promising area juniors who served as ball persons for the matches.

Before an estimated crowd of 2,000, Arthur Ashe and Clark Graebner won the opening singles to put the U.S. ahead 2-0 on Friday. Graebner defeated Richard Russell 6-1, 7-5, 6-2 and Ashe followed up with a 48-minute thrashing of Lance Lumsden 6-1, 6-1, 6-0. In Saturday's doubles rubber, Stan Smith and Bob Lutz handily defeated Russell and Lumsden 6-2, 6-3, 6-3 to clinch the tie for the United States. On Sunday, Ashe defeated Russell 6-3, 6-2, 6-4 and Lutz stepped in for the fifth match and beat Lumsden 6-0, 6-2, 6-1 to complete the American sweep.

The U.S. team followed up later in the year with victories over Mexico, Ecuador (avenging a disappointing loss to Ecuador the previous year), Spain, India, and Australia to win the Davis Cup.

Unfortunately, Richmond has been unable to attract another U.S. Davis Cup tie. Several concerted efforts by local tennis and civic leaders over the years have been unsuccessful. Undeterred, the RTA and other community leaders continue to pursue a bid to host another Davis Cup tie, and so it is perhaps only a matter of time before Davis Cup tennis returns to Richmond.

The 1968 U. S. Davis Cup team preparing for its match at Byrd Park.
Pictured from left: Dennis Ralston, Donald Dell, Bob Lutz (kneeling) and Charlie Pasarell.

Cup Competitions

By John Packett

In 1962, the combination of starting a new women's team competition and the opportunity to honor two of Richmond's most successful female tennis players created the Anderson Cup.

The Anderson Cup, which celebrated its 50th anniversary in 2011, was named for Penelope "Nip" Anderson McBride and her younger sister, Margaret "Peggy" Anderson Duval.

McBride made her mark on the national and international scene, while Duval won more women's city singles championships (seven) than anyone else.

> "The Anderson Cup represents to me a testament to good friendships and good tennis."
> — Betty Gustafson

Shelly Cabell, who was an assistant pro at the Country Club of Virginia, and head pro Fred Koechlein were responsible for getting the Anderson Cup started.

Four clubs were selected for the ladies' competition and they remain the same ones today. They are CCV, Farmington Country Club in Charlottesville, Norfolk Yacht and Country Club and Princess Anne Country Club in Virginia Beach.

2011 Anderson Cup championship team from CCV. (l to r front row) Elsie Bemiss, Betty Gustafsson, Mason Davis and Terry Whitworth [holding cup] (l to r back row) Ginny Wortham, Liza Wallace, Anne Garland, Katherine Mueller, Tom Wallace, Christine Douglas (hiding behind flowers) and Elizabeth Fraizer

CCV has held the trophy more times than any other club (25), while Norfolk is second with 20 titles. Farmington won three times and Princess Anne twice as of 2011.

"The Anderson Cup represents to me a testament to good friendships and good tennis," said former CCV player Betty Gustafson. "Each participant has felt the pride in club representation and the challenge of competitive tennis with good friends.

"The founders and the honorees would be thrilled to know that their dream has been sustained so beautifully."

Farmington claimed the first Anderson Cup, beating CCV 6-3 in the championship round at CCV. Duval played in that 1962 event. CCV won the most recent Anderson Cup in 2011, finishing three points ahead of Norfolk Yacht and CC in Norfolk in a round-robin format.

In 1967, Mary Belin from the Princess Anne CC donated the consolation trophy in memory of her father, Col. Harry Cootes.

"The Anderson Cup is a wonderful tribute to the Anderson sisters," said former CCV director of tennis Hal Burrows. "It makes me so happy that this great event has continued for 50 years. The relationship between the four clubs is special and the event is unique."

The site for the Anderson Cup rotates on an annual basis between the four clubs. It is believed to be the longest-running current Cup competition in Virginia.

Meanwhile, the Hotchkiss Trophy was another well-known annual competition, this one involving the leading men's players between the cities of Richmond, Norfolk, Baltimore and Washington, D.C. It began in 1921 and the final one was held in 1975. E.D. Hotchkiss, Jr. from CCV donated the trophy.

Richmond captured the final Hotchkiss Cup, beating Baltimore 6-3 in the title match. Tom Magner was the No. 1 player for Richmond and his teammates included O.H. Parrish, Rob Leitch, John Leitch, Chris Blair, Paul Dickinson, Tom Cain, Mark Vines and Neal Carl.

Hotchkiss Cup

"It was a really terrific match," recalled Rob Leitch. "We were up 3-2 in singles and O.H. was the last one on the court. He had developed cramps. He played the last set with cramps and managed to eke it out to give us a 4-2 lead and we went on to win it."

In the latter years of the competition, Norfolk standouts included Billy Brock and John Hill, while Washington players included Gene Russo and Fred Drilling. Baltimore's top player was Lenny Schloss.

"What happened was the pros had become part of the teams by then," said Rob Leitch. "Not only that, but the schedules of getting all the players and finding a date was not easy. We worked like heck the next year to find a date to hold it but nothing ever worked out."

"It was just a great event because you'd play two days and you'd have a nice dinner with the speeches in between. There was a lot of camaraderie among the players. It was a real shame that we weren't able to keep it going."

Washington dominated the event, winning it 30 times while Baltimore claimed it on 10 occasions.

Richmond's 1969 Hotchkiss Cup team included Westwood Club members (l to r): Richard McKee, Jr., O. H. Parrish, Eddie Phillips and Dick Makepeace. *Courtesy: Richmond Times-Dispatch*

Richmond won eight Cups, with the likes of Robert Cabell, Cliff Miller, Bobby Leitch, Virginius Dabney, Joe Kranitzky, Frank Hartz, Del Sylvia, Shelton Horsley, Bob Atwood, Bob Bortner, Bruce Sylvia, Tom Chewning, Bitsy Harrison, Massie Valentine, Spotty Hall, Dick Makepeace and Richard McKee contributing points over the years.

"The matches were always fun matches," said Horsley, a member of four winning teams, including back-to-back titles in 1964-65. "They were hotly contested. We were very competitive but we were good friends through the tennis world."

"It defied description the way Washington felt when they lost two in a row to us, I can tell you that."

In more recent times, the Virginia Cup has become a men's competition among CCV, Westwood Racquet Club, Princess Anne and Norfolk. Since joining the group four years ago, Westwood has won twice. Members of the 2011 Championship Team from Westwood were Clint Greene, III, Philip Gee, Sears Driscoll, Jimmy Aaron, Patrick Gee, Bradley Frohman, Paul Caldwell and Charles Einwick.

The Virginia Cup began in 1995 and initially included Greenbriar (W.Va.) Country Club. It started as a two-day event with singles and doubles but is now a one-day, doubles-only affair between mostly 5.0 players. Norfolk has won it 10 times, while CCV has claimed it twice.

The Spindle Cup, named for Kitty and Dick Spindle, has been held since 1996 and involves 4.0 rated female players from CCV, Princess Anne, Farmington and Norfolk. CCV has dominated these proceedings, capturing the Spindle Cup 10 times.

Anthem Challenge

By Eric Perkins

Tom Vozenilek began his term as RTA President in 1993 with bold and innovative plans for the organization. With such creative vision and determination at the helm backed by a strong supporting cast of passionate volunteers, the RTA reached new heights under his leadership, including a national award as USTA Organization of the Year, and the creation of a new event that would not only become one of the RTA's signature events and primary fundraisers, but also one of largest tennis events in Virginia—the Anthem Challenge.

The concept was simple. A three-day team competition with the largest tennis clubs in the area assembling doubles and mixed doubles teams and competing against one another at various NRTP levels. Each match victory earned two points for your club, while the losing team earned only one point. The team with the highest point total after the last round of 5.0/open level matches on Sunday would take home the prestigious Anthem Challenge championship trophy until the following year.

With NTRP rating-based USTA league tennis becoming increasing popular, the Anthem Challenge format had tremendous appeal with players from the very beginning. Every match carried the same point value regardless of whether the players were 3.0 or 5.0. In other words, under this format, the club with the best players at the 4.5 and 5.0 level had no meaningful advantage over clubs deep in numbers and talent at the 3.5 or 4.0 level.

The inaugural Trigon Club Challenge at the Westwood Club featured eight teams, with Briarwood (later ACAC) winning the first of its record seven Anthem Challenge titles. Over the years, only Westwood (five titles) and CCV (four titles) have managed to challenge ACAC's supremacy in the event, while every few years a surprise first-time winner emerges on Sunday afternoon (e.g., Woodlake in 1994, Raintree in 2002, and MAC in 2010). The field expanded first to 10 teams and then once more to its current field of 12 teams. Periodically, a local club or recreation association will request a challenge match to earn a spot into the competition. The club that finished last the preceding year must accept the challenge and win to keep its spot.

RTA leaders and club captains meet throughout the year to address format concerns and logistic issues. There were hotly contested debates in the early years over various aspects of the event, such as requirements that: all participants be RTA members, one club be responsible for post-event clean up, each club contribute $1,000 prize package for a silent auction, and that teams could earn additional bonus points boosting their team's score for performing various administrative tasks associated with the event. All such concerns were diplomatically addressed, and the administration of the Anthem Challenge has evolved to the point that it has become a relatively well-oiled machine with few controversies in recent memory (other than the random dress code violation or rare player disqualification for playing out of his or her NRTP rating level).

While various format and administrative details have changed over the years, the event has been blessed with the generous support of its title sponsor Anthem (formerly Trigon) and host club Westwood for the entire 19-year existence of the event. Not only is the Anthem Challenge one of the most anticipated events on the local tennis calendar each year, but due to the popularity of the event and the prestige associated with representing your club at the Anthem Challenge, many clubs are forced to hold special qualifying competitions for months leading up the fall event to determine who will make their team roster.

The team spirit, camaraderie, and fun are what make the Anthem Challenge such a unique and popular event, so much so that the RTA frequently gets calls from clubs and tennis organizations from around the country requesting advice on how to start such an event in their area. In recent years, the RTA has helped a group of smaller clubs and recreational associations establish a new team event (currently called the Autumn Cup) that uses a format identical to the Anthem Challenge.

Westwood becomes the center of attention of the local tennis community during Anthem Challenge weekend.

Midlothian Athletic Club celebrated its first Anthem Challenge victory in 2010.

ANTHEM CHALLENGE WINNERS

1993 Briarwood*
1994 Woodlake
1995 Briarwood
1996 Briarwood
1997 Briarwood
1998 Briarwood
1999 Westwood
2000 Briarwood
2001 Westwood
2002 Raintree
2003 CCV
2004 Westwood
2005 Westwood
2006 CCV
2007 CCV
2008 Westwood
2009 CCV
2010 Midlothian Athletic Club
2011 ACAC

*Briarwood, also more formally known as Riverside Wellness and Fitness Center-Briarwood, would later become known as ACAC (Atlantic Coast Athletic Club) prior to winning its 7th title in 2011.

CCV's Tom Wallace updates the official Anthem Challenge scoreboard.

Richmond Mayor Dwight C. Jones declared March 24, 2011 as "Tennis Night in Richmond." Over 750 children and volunteers enjoyed an evening of QuickStart Tennis at the Ashe Center.

Willow Oaks Country Club hosted "Tennis Night in America" festivities featuring QuickStart Tennis activities in 2010 and 2011.

CHAPTER 5

THE PRESENT AND FUTURE OF RICHMOND TENNIS

Best Tennis Town Contest

By Eric Perkins

The USTA sponsored a national contest in 2010 to crown the "Best Tennis Town" in America. At its January 2010 board meeting, the RTA made a commitment to mount a campaign to demonstrate to the rest of the world why Richmond is a great tennis community.

Preparing an application for the contest required a monumental effort. Letters of recommendation from the Mayor's office and local business and government officials were required as part of the application process, along with 10+ pages of narrative descriptions and disclosures concerning local tennis facilities, programs, organizations, and history. Most intriguing was the requirement that the RTA team, led by Eric Perkins, Tom Hood and Lisa Deane, produce a five-minute video demonstrating why Richmond is the "Best Tennis Town." (The video titled "2010 Best Tennis Town Finalist: Richmond, VA" can be found on YouTube.) With creative and technical assistance from local media professionals Tom Ager, Sera Tabb, and Edward Baldwin and contributions by dozens of supporters throughout the local tennis community, the RTA team—with valuable input from Lou Einwick, Hugh Waters, Paddi Valentine, Ward Hamilton, Cris Robinson, among many others—scripted, produced, and edited a three and a half minute video showcasing the past, present, and future of Richmond tennis.

Well over 100 hours of work went into preparing the application materials, including some last-minute drama on the eve of the submission deadline when it was discovered that Richmond's spot in the contest had been reserved by someone else early in the sign-up period. Fortunately, the situation was resolved with a few emails and phone calls, and Richmond's application was submitted by the deadline (with a few hours to spare).

A national panel of judges reviewed over 80 applications submitted by communities from across the country. Based upon the quality and creativity of the applications, the judges narrowed the field down to the top ten cities, which were announced in mid-July. Making the top ten were Richmond, Virginia; Atlanta, Georgia; Charleston, South Carolina; Beaverton, Oregon; Clearwater, Florida; Snow Hill, North Carolina; Delray Beach, Florida; Rome, Georgia; Manchester Center, Vermont; and Rosemount, Minnesota.

From there, the contest was decided online by popular vote over a two-week period. All of Richmond—the tennis and business communities, local government, local media, the nonprofit community, VCU, University of Richmond—rallied behind the effort and campaigned for votes from all corners of the globe. At the end of the voting period, Richmond was announced as one of the top three finalists (along with Atlanta and Charleston) and invited to Arthur Ashe Stadium on Labor Day Monday during the U.S. Open, at which an announcement would be made as to which city had won the Best Tennis Town title. A contingent of local leaders and supporters, including Richmond City Council Vice President Ellen Robertson, were on hand for the announcement—all clad in bright yellow shirts specially designed for the festive occasion.

Richmond took home third place (Charleston won the top prize), and Richmond's impressive showing was awarded with $25,000 to support community tennis programming and facilities. More importantly, the campaign generated a great deal of publicity and positive energy for not just the local tennis community, but all of Richmond. The effort strengthened relationships throughout the community and would ultimately prove to be a catalyst for other great things to come for Richmond tennis.

RTA President Eric Perkins, USTA President Lucy Garvin and Ellen Robertson, Richmond City Council Vice President, pose with the Best Tennis Town 3rd place award in Arthur Ashe Stadium during the U.S. Open on Labor Day 2010.

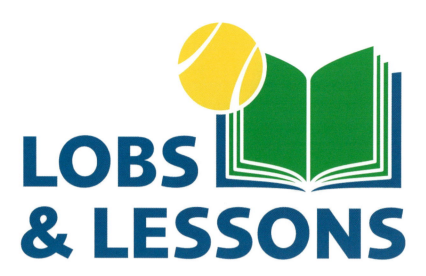

By Eric Perkins

The Lobs & Lessons story begins in 2000, when Virginia Commonwealth University leaders helped establish *Advantage: Richmond* (later rebranded as *Advantage: Virginia*), an ambitious, high-powered nonprofit initiative intended to elevate Richmond to world-class status in the tennis world. The organization quickly assembled an all-star advisory board of over two dozen community and business leaders ranging from then-VCU President Eugene Trani to John McEnroe.

The group identified two primary strategic goals:

1. Building a world-class tennis facility, featuring both indoor and outdoor courts, that would enable Richmond to host major tennis events (professional, collegiate, USTA-sanctioned tournaments, USTA national and sectional league championships). Organizers were confident that such a facility would have a tremendous economic impact on Richmond while generating national publicity in the process.

2. Developing a youth tennis academy to be coordinated by the VCU Athletics Department, Community Outreach Department, and the City of Richmond. The academy would provide tennis instruction, tutoring, and mentoring to build teamwork, sportsmanship, and discipline among Richmond youth.

While plans for a major tennis center hit a few snags and were ultimately put on hold, by early 2004, Trani and VCU Athletic Director Richard Sander were having a series of discussions with Michael and Elizabeth Fraizer focused on the development of a youth mentoring program. Inspired by Andre Agassi's sports-oriented boys and girls mentoring organization that operated from a club-type facility, which later evolved into his now world-famous charter school in Las Vegas, Nevada, the Fraizers determined that a similar program could be started in Richmond in conjunction with the William Byrd Community House, which was adjacent to the Monroe Park Campus. In 2004, the Genworth Financial Chairman, President and CEO received an award from General Electric's chairman as part of a series of awards given out at the company's annual management meeting that brought with it the ability to direct a donation to a charity of his choosing. So the Fraizers directed this award and some additional funds to finance the start-up costs of Lobs & Lessons in April 2004 working with the William Byrd Community House.

Starting as a small pilot program in the fall of 2004, 40 children from the William Byrd Community House were exposed to the five core values of the Lobs & Lessons program:

- Getting along with others
- Regulating emotion
- Being coachable
- Practicing healthy habits
- Learning the sport of tennis

In 2005, discussions among the Fraizers, Dr. Sander, and Kathleen Bowles, the first executive director of Lobs & Lessons, focused on the development of a tennis facility and finding a permanent home for Lobs & Lessons so it could achieve more independence and program flexibility. At one brainstorming dinner meeting at what was then The Graffiti Grille, the basic concept of what would ultimately become the Mary and Frances Youth Center was born—literally sketched on the back of a cocktail napkin. The plan was as simple as it was brilliant—identify an unused parcel on the VCU campus large enough for a facility to host the new Lobs & Lessons program. The proximity to VCU students and other facilities would ensure that the program would become an integral part of the university community while enjoying the independence and flexibility of operating from its own facility.

By late September 2005, a site was identified just across the street from where the Mary and Frances Youth Center is located today. The Fraizers contributed $1.5 million for construction costs plus an additional $100,000 to seed the program and other fund-raising assistance. VCU brought to the table the programs, the land, a tremendous facilities team and design support to help make the dream a reality.

Over 200 children and volunteers made the inaugural Young Aces Open a huge success in April 2010.

The groundbreaking ceremony occurred in December 2006 and was attended by Andre Agassi, Stefanie Graf, James Blake and Lindsay Davenport. The Mary and Frances Youth Center opened September 28, 2007, having been completed in record time given the focus of the founding principals involved. The center is named after the mothers of Michael and Elizabeth Fraizer—Mary Fraizer and Frances Royer—two women who were great believers in giving back to their community, particularly as it related to children. "We lost them too early, so the least we could do was to honor their spirit," commented Fraizer, "as we said at the opening ceremony, they are up there smiling down on all of us."

At its grand opening the original Lobs & Lessons community partners that brought various youth groups included the William Byrd Community House, Sacred Heart Center and Northside YMCA. Armed with two beautiful hard courts and an adjacent two-story facility featuring classrooms, office space, computer lab and meeting rooms, the Mary and Frances Youth Center was open for business—the business of promoting tennis, education and life skills to elementary and middle school children. Through an ever-growing list of strategic partners throughout the community, ongoing support from the VCU community, and a strong volunteer base, the Lobs & Lessons program offers a year-round schedule of after-school and summer programming.

Shima and Joe Grover are among the most active volunteers in the Richmond tennis community.

In 2009, the Mary and Frances Youth Center and Lobs & Lessons took another step forward with a link to QuickStart Tennis. Dismayed to hear news of the removal of some sports programs from the Richmond Public Schools because of budget pressures, the Fraizers and VCU

An aerial view of the 38 QuickStart courts set up by Lobs & Lessons and students from the VCU Center for Sports Leadership (meticulously lined with baby powder) for the 2010 Young Aces Open.

officials took action to introduce QuickStart Tennis equipment, training and programming in the Richmond Public Schools with the strong support of School Superintendent Dr. Yvonne Brandon and the Richmond Tennis Association.

As an organizational member of the USTA and a chapter of the National Junior Tennis and Learning ("NJTL"), Lobs & Lessons has emerged as a leader in the creation and promotion of 10 and Under Tennis programming and events, such as the nationally acclaimed Young Aces Open. First held in 2010 under the leadership of new Executive Director Tina Carter, the Young Aces Open is a one-day QuickStart Tennis event that culminates the city-wide program introducing the QuickStart Tennis format into the physical education curricula at all of the elementary schools in the City of Richmond Public School System. With significant support from the VCU Center for Sport Leadership, the annual Young Aces Open has been featured on the Tennis Channel and at USTA workshops across the country as a model for other communities to follow.

In 2011, Lobs & Lessons hosted the inaugural Family Open, Richmond's first parent-child event utilizing the QuickStart Tennis format. Nearly 200 players and volunteers enjoyed a fun-filled morning of tennis, games, food, and prizes. Meanwhile, Lobs & Lessons has continued to expand its core after-school and summer programs, making a positive difference in the lives of more children than ever, firmly establishing itself as a leader in the tennis and nonprofit communities. Their efforts have not gone unnoticed. In January 2012, Lobs & Lessons was announced as a national NJTL chapter of the year award winner.

10 and Under Tennis and the QuickStart Tennis Format

By Eric Perkins

As this book goes to print in early 2012, American tennis is in the early stages of a revolution as to how new players, particularly kids aged 10 and under, are being taught to play. Following an example set by other nations for several decades, the USTA has invested millions in 10 and Under Tennis program development, education, and marketing resources to promote the QuickStart Tennis format.

The concept is simple—kid-size the sport to make tennis easier to learn and more fun to play. Shorter rackets, smaller tennis courts, and slower, softer tennis balls are components of QuickStart Tennis. The new equipment is now available at major retail chains like Wal-Mart and Target. New teaching techniques, drills, and games have been developed and endorsed by the nation's top teaching professionals.

The QuickStart Tennis Format is revolutionizing the way kids learn to play tennis today.

The International Tennis Federation and the USTA have amended the rules and regulations governing tennis to make room for QuickStart Tennis. Beginning in 2012, all 10 and under sanctioned tournaments are required to utilize the QuickStart Tennis format. Public and private tennis facilities all over the country are painting QuickStart lines on their courts and in some cases permanently converting traditional 78-foot courts to either 60-foot or 36-foot QuickStart courts.

Richmond has been at the forefront of the QuickStart revolution from the start. In the early 2000s, the Association of Richmond Tennis Professionals developed a series of alternative format, one-day tournaments for juniors relatively new to the sport. QuickStart formats were soon incorporated into the 10 and under and 8 and under divisions for the younger players and the ARTP circuit quickly grew to over a thousand participants over the course of a typical summer.

In the fall of 2009, QuickStart Tennis was introduced into the physical education programs at every elementary school in the City of Richmond Public School System. Funded by a generous donation from Michael and Elizabeth Fraizer, the schools were provided all the necessary QuickStart Tennis equipment and supplies. Local tennis pros Cris and Melissa Robinson led training workshops for the P.E. teachers. With additional volunteer support and assistance from USTA/Mid-Atlantic, USTA/Virginia, the RTA, Lobs & Lessons and the local ladies suburban league, the program has been a tremendous success, with thousands of children being introduced to QuickStart Tennis.

Lobs & Lessons took Richmond QuickStart Tennis to new heights in April 2010 with the inaugural Young Aces Open, featuring over 150 children playing QuickStart Tennis on 38 courts on a practice field on the Virginia Commonwealth University campus. Lauded by the USTA as a best practice for other communities to follow, the event was also featured on the Tennis Channel as one the largest QuickStart events in the nation. Heading into its third year in 2012, the Young Aces Open continues to grow with support from the local tennis and business communities.

In March 2011, Richmond hosted two "Tennis Night in America" extravaganzas at Willow Oaks Country Club and the Ashe Center featuring QuickStart Tennis, guest pro appearances, local celebrities, food, music and prizes for over 1,500 attendees. Richmond tennis legend Rodney Harmon and former WTA pro Katrina Adams led a QuickStart Tennis clinic at Battery Park on a chilly Sunday morning for over 40 excited juniors.

QuickStart tournament at Battery Park

The following month the RTA hosted a business meeting of Richmond tennis community leaders at Willow Oaks Country Club where national, sectional, and state tennis officials gave a compelling presentation on the USTA's 10 and Under Tennis initiative and its potential, including grant opportunities available to fund court conversions and other facility improvements. Within weeks, the Westwood Club became the first local facility to paint QuickStart lines on four of its outdoor hard courts. Other clubs soon followed suit, and the City of Richmond has approved the addition of QuickStart lines on courts at numerous public tennis facilities.

The RTA and City of Richmond Parks, Recreation, and Community Facilities Department worked together to organize a new series of low-cost tournaments featuring QuickStart Tennis that saw several hundred juniors get their first exposure to competitive tennis.

Smaller courts, shorter rackets and softer balls make QuickStart Tennis easier to learn and more fun to play.

With the encouragement of USTA/Virginia Executive Director Janine Underwood, in August 2011 the RTA applied for a grant and designation as a national target market for the development and promotion of 10 and Under Tennis. In a surprise announcement at the USTA/Virginia Annual Meeting at the Country Club of Virginia in October, USTA/Virginia President Wayne McCoy confirmed that the USTA had selected Richmond as a national target market and awarded a $100,000 grant to the RTA to support the development of 10 and Under Tennis throughout the community. Working closely with USTA/Mid-Atlantic and USTA/Virginia staff, the RTA has exciting plans for the future of Richmond junior tennis.

Armed with seed capital, a committed volunteer base, and tremendous relationships with local government and community partners as well as community tennis leaders at the state, sectional, and national levels, Richmond is poised to emerge once again as a national hotbed of junior tennis.

The 2011 Young Aces Open was billed as the largest QuickStart Tennis event in the world.